St. Paul's Historic Summit Avenue

View of entrance doors from the first floor hall of the James J. Hill House

St. Paul's Historic Summit Avenue

Ernest R. Sandeen

With the assistance of Margaret Redpath and Carol Sawyer

Foreword by Larry Millett

 University of Minnesota Press   Minneapolis · London

The Fesler-Lampert Minnesota Heritage Book Series

This series reprints significant books that enhance our understanding and appreciation of Minnesota and the Upper Midwest. It is supported by the generous assistance of the John K. and Elsie Lampert Fesler Fund and the interest and contribution of Elizabeth P. Fesler and the late David R. Fesler.

Frontispiece photograph courtesy of the Library of Congress, Prints and Photographs Division, HABS MINN, 62-SAIPA, 15-3

Fitzgerald's description of Summit Avenue on pages 93–94 is taken from F. Scott Fitzgerald, *The Crack-Up*. Copyright 1945 by New Directions Publishing Corporation. Reprinted by permission of New Directions Publishing Corporation.

Copyright 1978 by Ernest R. Sandeen
Foreword copyright 2004 by Larry Millett

First published by the Living Historical Museum, 1978
First University of Minnesota Press edition, 2004

Published by the University of Minnesota Press
111 Third Avenue South, Suite 290
Minneapolis, MN 55401-2520
http://www.upress.umn.edu

Library of Congress Cataloging-in-Publication Data

Sandeen, Ernest Robert, 1931–1982
     St. Paul's historic Summit Avenue / Ernest R. Sandeen ; with the assistance of Margaret Redpath and Carol Sawyer ; foreword by Larry Millett.
        p.   cm. — (The Fesler-Lampert Minnesota heritage book series)
     Includes bibliographical references and index.
     ISBN 0-8166-4409-8 (PB : alk. paper)
     1. Summit Avenue (St. Paul, Minn.)   2. Historic buildings—Minnesota—St. Paul.   3. Architecture—Minnesota—
St. Paul.   4. St. Paul (Minn.)—Buildings, structures, etc.   5. St. Paul (Minn.)—History.   6. Summit Avenue (St. Paul, Minn.)—Tours.   7. St. Paul (Minn.)—Tours.   I. Redpath, Margaret.   II. Sawyer, Carol.   III. Title.   IV. Series.
     F614.S4S26 2004
     977.6'581—dc22
                                                                                                                    2003026338

Printed in the United States of America on acid-free paper

The University of Minnesota is an equal-opportunity educator and employer.

12 11 10 09 08 07 06 05 04   10 9 8 7 6 5 4 3 2 1

Contents

Foreword

Larry Millett

Summit Avenue in St. Paul is one of America's most remarkable streets—and not only because of its great houses and churches. What makes Summit so extraordinary is that, almost alone among American streets of its kind, it has managed to retain its essential character through more than a century of urban upheaval. Its one-time rivals in residential grandeur (Euclid Avenue in Cleveland, Prairie Avenue in Chicago, Park Avenue in Minneapolis) now offer isolated remnants of their former glory. Battered by ill-advised urban renewal projects and the hard hand of time, they preside over lost urban worlds. Summit, by contrast, has not only survived largely intact but continues to flourish.

In fact, it is fair to say that the avenue has never looked better or been more completely integrated into the life of St. Paul than it is today. Builders eagerly snap up the few available lots for expensive new houses, apartments, and town homes. Scores of old mansions have been beautifully refurbished. There's even a new copper roof gleaming atop the avenue's mightiest monument, the Cathedral of St. Paul. On pleasant days, the avenue becomes the city's central promenade: strollers, roller bladers, and bicyclists roam up and down its four-and-a-half-mile length, while automobiles filled with gawking out-of-towners cruise slowly, irking local drivers in a hurry.

Surely, the late Ernest Sandeen deserves a good share of the credit for this modern flowering of the avenue. *St. Paul's Historic Summit Avenue,* which Sandeen first published in 1978, was in every respect a groundbreaking work. Coming at a time when the avenue's future as a grand residential showcase was by no means assured, the book was both a wonderful history and an urgent plea for preservation. Scholarly yet accessible, it set a new standard for the writing of local history in St. Paul. To this day it remains one of the finest books ever written about the city.

Before Sandeen's work appeared, Summit had been the subject of much anecdotal history and personal reminiscence but little in the way of serious scholarly research. Aided by a corps of student assistants and researchers, Sandeen changed that, presenting Summit Avenue with the gift of its own history. Sandeen also undertook pioneering investigations into the work of prominent architects who built houses along the avenue. He was among the first local scholars to delve into the early careers of Cass Gilbert and Clarence Johnston, two designers who left significant legacies on Summit (and elsewhere in the Twin Cities).

St. Paul's Historic Summit Avenue is important in another respect. Published at a crucial point in the avenue's history, it stamped a sort of scholarly imprimatur on the notion that Summit is unique not just in the Twin Cities but in the nation. David Lanegran, a colleague of Sandeen's at Macalester

College in St. Paul, was the first scholar to point out how rare a jewel Summit Avenue had become by the 1970s. Sandeen drove this point home at the very beginning of his book. "St. Paul's Summit Avenue," he wrote, "stands as the best-preserved American example of the Victorian monumental residential boulevard." Today, this statement has become all but embedded in the city's consciousness. Everyone in St. Paul, it seems, recognizes that Summit is something special.

That belief, however, was not always as widespread as it is today. Back in the mid-1970s, when Sandeen wrote, Summit's future was very much up for grabs. A number of absurdly inappropriate modern tract houses had already been built on the avenue at that time, while some of its largest and most historic mansions were functioning as de facto apartment houses. The avenue, it appeared, was teetering between re-invigoration on one hand and a kind of slow, perhaps even fatal, decline on the other.

St. Paul in those days was just beginning to build a strong preservation movement. True, the battle to save what is now Landmark Center had already been fought and won, but elsewhere—especially in downtown's central core—wrecking crews were still busily at work. Although few Summit Avenue properties were in immediate danger, Sandeen noted that zoning controls (to limit the subdividing of houses into apartments) were essential to maintain the avenue's integrity. Otherwise, he feared, Summit might go the way of the storied avenues in other cities that had already been decimated by abandonment and decay.

These concerns led Sandeen to sound an urgent call for action. "What seems tragic at this point in history," he wrote, "is the assumption of helplessness and impotence which seems to grip property owners, city officials, neighborhood groups, and the general public. If the glory and beauty of Summit Avenue are ever lost, let no one fall back on the feeble excuse that the dead hand of tradition and the complexities of an ancient law made preservation impossible."

Today, these words seem almost quaint. All of Summit is now a protected historic district, governed by guidelines that control what can and cannot be built. As a result, it is now hard to imagine any major change on Summit Avenue that would *not* entail rigorous and passionate public debate. Summit enjoys a citywide constituency of supporters who care deeply about the avenue and its preservation. *St. Paul's Historic Summit Avenue* remains this constituency's essential document, for which all of us owe Sandeen and his assistants a debt of gratitude.

How Sandeen came to write this book is a story in itself. It is one of two books (the other is *The Lake District of Minneapolis,* by Sandeen and Lanegran) published in the late 1970s by the Living Historical Museum. The museum was a program founded at Macalester by Sandeen and Lanegran, both professors at the college. One of the program's goals was to help St. Paulites see their city as a special place. In this regard *St. Paul's Historic Summit Avenue* was a signal success. Equally important, the book was a catalyst that helped ignite a new generation of scholarship about St. Paul and its history.

Sandeen's book is much more than a timely historic artifact. It remains a superb feat of research and a delightful read. Much of the book's continuing appeal stems from the fact that it isn't a standard architectural or social history. It's more like an anatomy of the avenue. As such, it covers everything from the avenue's architecture to its zoning regulations to its links with the life of F. Scott Fitzgerald. The book also offers a walking tour and an invaluable appendix in the form of a data base that presents vital information on every building along the avenue. Not surprisingly, some of the information gathered by Sandeen and his researchers is now out of date, largely because of the mini–building boom on Summit in recent years. But the book is still a valuable guide to history that can be appreciated today.

Architectural history can be mind-numbing stuff—a parade of styles and influences delivered in language bristling with arcane terminology. Fortunately, Sandeen would have none of that. Although he had decidedly unorthodox ideas about architectural style, he was a gracious and inviting writer. Reading this book is like walking down Summit with a master teacher at your side. Sandeen's knowledge of and love for the great avenue shine through on every page, and he wants you, the reader, to share his enthusiasm.

A Note to Readers

In the intervening years since this book was originally published, many changes have been made to Summit Avenue, despite its remarkable level of preservation. Several buildings described in this book have been renovated, single-family dwellings have been converted to apartments and condominiums (and vice versa), and general use and ownership have changed over time.

A few specific corrections should be pointed out:

Page 3: A photograph of the Noble House does exist in the James J. Hill Reference Library.

Page 22: The Wilder House and the James J. Hill mansion were not built in the same year. The Hill mansion was built between 1888 and 1891.

Page 30: The City of St. Paul's most recent zoning revision was in 1988.

Page 41: The copper roof of the Cathedral of St. Paul was replaced in 2002.

Page 43: The James J. Hill mansion contains forty-two rooms, twenty-two fireplaces, and thirteen bathrooms. It does not have a ballroom.

Page 44: The artisan who performed a substantial amount of the woodcarving in the James J. Hill mansion is misidentified. While it's conceivable a William Yungbauer contributed to the building's interior, the documented primary woodcarver was John Kirchmayer, a native of Oberammergau, Bavaria, who had established a workshop in Cambridge, Massachusetts. Kirchmayer also built furniture for the mansion.

Page 81: For more information about Clarence Johnston, see Paul Clifford Larson, *Minnesota Architect: The Life and Work of Clarence H. Johnston* (Afton: Afton Historical Society Press, 1996).

A stairpost finial in the Burbank-Livingston-Griggs house, 432 Summit. The house is regularly open to the public (Brian Wicklund, Living Historical Museum).

St. Paul's Historic Summit Avenue

CHAPTER 1

The Earliest History of Summit Avenue

S T. PAUL'S Summit Avenue, a monumental boulevard of houses, churches, synagogues, and schools, stretches four and one half miles from the Cathedral to the Mississippi River. The best-known avenue in St. Paul, it attracts tourists and natives alike, who stroll, bicycle, and drive past its architectural curiosities and landmarks. There are thirteen churches and nine schools on the avenue, and since 1855, when Edward Duffield Neill built the first house on the bluff, there have been 440 residences constructed, of which 373 survive. Since many newer houses were constructed on the site of older ones, few vacant properties exist, and the panorama of the avenue remains little altered from the 1920s.

Streets like Summit Avenue were not uncommon in the nineteenth century. Prairie Avenue in Chicago, Euclid Avenue in Cleveland, Park Avenue in Minneapolis, or Fifth Avenue in New York were all similar, if not even grander than Summit. But in most American cities, including all of those just catalogued, these typically nineteenth-century thoroughfares have completely lost their character; except for St. Paul, it is difficult to discover any large city in which this kind of streetscape remains intact. Thus, St. Paul's Summit Avenue stands as the best-preserved American example of the Victorian monumental residential boulevard.

Already by the early 1850s, before Minnesota had become a state, promoters were predicting that the bluffs over the town would soon be crowned by mansions. "Nature never planned a spot better adapted to build up a showy and delightful display of architecture and gardening than that natural terrace of hills," wrote J. Wesley Bond in 1853. Quoting a fellow enthusiast, he went on, "Indeed, we seem to behold even now, through the dim vista of future years, the glittering mansions of St. Paul's merchant-princes rising up in every direction, on these hills now in a state of nature or rudely adorned by the humble *chaumiere* [cottages] of the French and half-breeds, or the simple lodges of the noble Sioux." Before Minnesota was admitted to the union in 1858, that wild prediction had begun to come true.

The Dogsled Photograph

The dogsled photo is the most important single piece of evidence available to the historian attempting to reconstruct the early history of Summit Avenue. The Minnesota Historical Society has determined that the photograph was taken about 1859. In the foreground stand two drivers, Tarbell and Campbell, with their dogsled and a little boy who, we may presume, was posing only

The cupola of the Burbank-Livingston-Griggs house, 432 Summit, the second oldest house still standing on the avenue (Al Ominsky, Minnesota Historical Society).

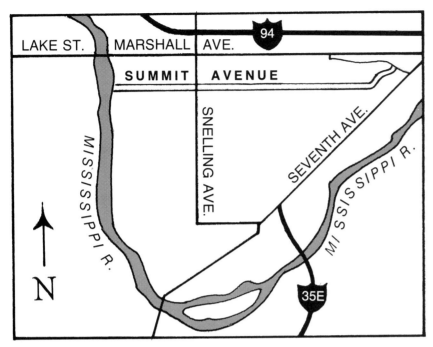

Summit Avenue stretches four and one half miles from the Cathedral of St. Paul to the Mississippi River.

Edward Duffield Neill's house was the earliest residence to be built on the bluff (Macalester College archives).

temporarily as a member of the group. Behind the men one can see a bridge over one of the many little streams which once trickled from springs at the base of the bluff. Beyond the bridge, Walnut Street moves away to the viewer's right until it ends in the earliest form of the Walnut Street steps, seen as a dark slash climbing the slope to a spot behind the first house on the bluff. The building behind the head of the little boy is the first House of Hope Presbyterian Church, now located at the corner of Summit and Avon. The dogsled is entering the city of St. Paul along what was then called Fort Street and today is known as Seventh Street, finishing a long trek from Pembina on the Red River close to the Canadian border.

It is remarkable that this casual photo should survive to give us such a dramatic view of the six earliest houses built on Summit Avenue. After considerable historical sleuthing, all of them have been successfully identified and dated. On the far right-hand margin of the picture stands the residence of Edward Duffield Neill, in the late 1850s the pastor of the House of Hope Presbyterian Church. The best available photograph of the house is annotated in Neill's own handwriting, "First House built on Summit Avenue, St. Paul, between Dayton Avenue and Walnut Street, site now occupied by mansion of James J. Hill." Neill was undoubtedly correct; he purchased lots 4 and 5 of block 70, Dayton and Irvine's Addition in 1854, and took out a mortgage in 1855, presumably to finance construction. Holmes Andrews' panorama of St. Paul painted in 1855 shows his house perched in solitary isolation on the bluff. In Neill's own photograph (taken from the north side and not the bluff side) Neill and his family are seen posed in front of his stylish bracketed Italian villa, a house that looks as if it might have come right from the pages of Andrew J. Downing's *Architecture of Country Houses*. The walls seem to be constructed of smooth-faced, possibly sawn limestone blocks, similar to but more regular than those used in the Sibley House in Mendota. The house was razed in 1886.

The next house pictured in the dogsled photograph was built by the Noble family. The deeds show the owners to have been William and Angelina Noble, but the city directories list the occupant as "O. J. Noble,

Pioneer photographer Joel Whitney in 1859 recorded the earliest construction on the bluff (Minnesota Historical Society).

miller." The house seems to have been constructed in the summer of 1857, just before the effect of the panic was felt. By 1860 the family had defaulted on their mortgage, and the property was sold at sheriff's auction, although the Nobles continued living there until 1870 when the George Palmes family bought the property. Although Palmes lived there until 1902, when the house was razed to make way for Louis Hill's residence, no other photographs of the house are known to exist.

The third house in the dogsled picture was built in 1857 by Henry F. Masterson, who also came to grief. In this case the recollections of Rebecca Marshall Cathcart give real dimension to life on Summit Avenue:

> The panic did not materially affect Mr. Cathcart's business until 1862, when he compromised with his creditors, by giving or assigning to them all his property, and continued to carry on his dry goods store, the largest one in the city. We removed from our homestead on Summit avenue, between Rice and St. Peter streets, to another house on Summit avenue near where James J. Hill now lives. This house was built by Mr. Masterson, a young lawyer, who went East and brought back his bride to this far Western home, but his visions of happiness disappeared within two years, as his wife died; the house was closed, and it was not again occupied until we moved into it in the spring of 1863. . . . Summit avenue was a lonely place at this time. Between it and Selby avenue stood a dense forest of native oaks, and the few houses were separated by large, unoccupied grounds. Many and many a night, after the Indian massacre of 1862, have I lain awake listening for the Indian warwhoop, and thinking how easily they could come through the woods and kill us all.

The Masterson house was sold in 1870 to Earle S. Goodrich, editor of the *Pioneer*, and his newspaper reported on January 1, 1873, that Goodrich was spending $12,000

Holmes Andrews' 1855 panoramic painting of St. Paul shows Edward Duffield Neill's house perched high on the bluff in the upper left corner (Minnesota Historical Society).

to improve his dwelling. The illustration in the 1874 Andreas *Atlas* (p. 7) shows us how the remodeling turned out. In Chapter 6, I shall discuss the reasons for describing the new style as Vernacular Second Empire. The ornate, high-pitched, curbed roof was popular with St. Paul residents during the early 1870s. Comparison of the dogsled photo with the illustration from the Andreas *Atlas* indicates just what kind of work Goodrich commissioned in order to bring the house up to fashionable level. In spite of that effort, the property was sold in 1882 to Frederick Driscoll, who razed the house in order to build a yet more fashionable one which still stands at 266 Summit Avenue.

The fourth house in the dogsled photo was built by Henry M. Rice, pioneer businessman and one of the first senators from Minnesota. His house must have been con-

structed at just about the same time as Edward Duffield Neill's, because the celebration of his election as territorial delegate to Congress in October 1855 culminated outside his house on the bluff. Rice's house appears to have been smaller than the others, an opinion confirmed by the sketch of the house which appeared in the 1867 *Map of Ramsey County*; the sketch, however, is of such poor quality that it would be unfair to generalize about the house on the basis of that evidence. Rice lived in this house until 1882, when he sold the property and moved into a new house across the street at 285 Summit. The new owner, A. B. Stickney, demolished Rice's old house and built a new house on the site.

The fifth house on the dogsled photo, unlike most of the others, was built in 1858 after the panic of 1857 had hit the city. Henry Neill Paul must have constructed his square Italian villa soon after buying the property in July 1858, but by the time the house was pictured in the 1867 *Map of Ramsey County*, it had passed into the hands of Henry Blandy. The house stood until 1919, when it was razed to make way for the Lindsay house which now stands at 294 Summit.

The last house pictured on the photo still stands today at 312 Summit Avenue; it is, thus, the oldest house on Summit Avenue and one of the oldest houses in St. Paul. As the photo shows, the house was a rambling Italian villa complete with cupola, a feature which it has since lost. The house was built by David Stuart, a partner in the Stuart and Cobb lumber business, probably in 1858; Stuart died in that same year, the mortgage was foreclosed, and the property sold at sheriff's auction in 1860 (the first of three such sales of the property during the Civil War). Additional photographs and information about the house are found in the walking tour (p. 55–56).

The Myth of Farmhouse Architecture

This first cluster of houses can hardly be said to have stood on Summit Avenue, since there was really no road worthy of the name running along the bluff at that time. These were isolated houses, seats of "country gentlemen" — virtually rural retreats. They were not, however, farmsteads. Many St. Paul residents mistakenly assume that much of the area through which Summit Avenue passes was surveyed and sold as farmland and that many of the oldest houses now standing in this section of the city were originally farmhouses. It is true that Henry M. Rice's first house on the avenue was sited in the midst of 120 acres which he is reputed to have called his "farm," and that Henry Sibley's block of land behind the Cathedral was commonly referred to as Sibley Farm, but "farm" in this sense implied only that the owner was maintaining a large estate in contrast to the usual city lot in the older sections of town. Many persons, of course, even in town, kept chickens and even a cow or two, and every prosperous citizen owned horses.

There really is no such thing as farmhouse architecture. American Midwestern farmhouses did not differ from town houses, but followed the same fads and styles that were popular in the cities. The houses which

A. J. Downing's Architecture of Country Houses (1850) *provided plans and sketches which popularized the villa or suburban house.*

twentieth-century residents assume to be farmhouses are almost invariably frame houses built in the late 1870s and early 1880s without much of a cellar so that the house is several feet closer to the ground than houses with full basements. Ironically, one of the few *bona fide* farmhouses that exists today, the Frederick Spangenburg house, 375 Mount Curve, is not often recognized as a farmhouse because it is built of stone and does not conform to the mistaken stereotype of the clapboard farmhouse.

The Inaccessible Hill District

For several decades it appeared that the early promise of Summit Avenue recorded in the dogsled photograph might not be fulfilled. As the chart of building-starts

Henry Rice's house was not very skillfully delineated in Bennett's Map of Ramsey County *(1867). The* Minnesota Democrat *recorded an election night celebration which ended at Rice's house.*

Democratic Glorification.

On Saturday evening, a procession composed of two or three hundred persons, left the Winslow House, and proceeded to the residence of Hon. HENRY M. RICE, to tender him their congratulations on the glorious result of the recent election in this Territory. The procession was accompanied by two bands of music, and in the front a large illuminated transparency was carried, on which was inscribed the following mottoes:—

"HENRY M. RICE, THE FRIEND OF MINNESOTA."

"NO TRUE HEARTED AMERICAN CAN BE A KNOW NOTHING."—H. M. RICE.

"SQUATTER SOVEREIGNTY TRIUMPHANT—THE RIGHT OF THE PEOPLE TO SELF-GOVERNMENT VINDICATED."

"HONESTY AND TRUTH HAVE TRIUMPHED."

The arrival of the procession at Mr. RICE's house, was announced by a splendid display of fire-works from the bluff, and the loud booming of a cannon. After the national air had been performed by the band, Mr. RICE was called out; he was received with tremendous cheering, but declined making a speech, owing to indisposition. He introduced Mr. GEORGE L. BECKER, who congratulated in eloquent terms, those present, on the recent victory which had been achieved. It was not the triumph alone of Mr. RICE, over disorganizers and Abolitionists, but a great and memorable success of the National Democracy.

R. R. NELSON, Col. IRWIN, WM. P. MURRAY, D. A. J. BAKER, and Mr. M'BEAN, of Little Canada, also made congratulatory speeches, which were received with great enthusiasm.

After spending some time at the residence of Mr. RICE, the procession returned to the city, and soon afterwards dispersed.

indicates, in the twenty-seven years after the building of the Neill and Rice houses, only twenty-four additional Summit Avenue residences were built; only in 1858, 1863, and 1874 was more than one built in a single year. With a few noteworthy exceptions, such as James Burbank's impressive Italian villa built at 432 Summit (the second oldest house still standing on Summit), most of these were relatively small structures. On the wooded plains behind the bluff, now known as the Historic Hill District, there was even less construction. In 1871 Giles W. Merrill built a house at 669 Laurel Avenue. Looking west from his house he claimed that he could see only two other dwellings.

There were no roads or streets leading to my home then. We simply lived in the country. In the early eighties streets began to be laid out and people gradually settled about us.

Rollin A. Lanpher, a Masonic brother of Merrill's, built a house at the corner of Dayton and Western in 1873. The area was not popular because the bluff blocked access to that area. Lanpher wrote:

It was difficult to get into the hill district from down town; there was then no Oakland avenue, and no Ramsey street. We reached our homes either by going up Third street hill, or by going first to Rice street and then up Summit avenue. In winter it was especially hard.

E. S. Goodrich had just completed remodeling his house at 266 Summit when it was sketched for the Andreas Atlas *(1874).*

Even after the establishment of a mule-car line into the district, transportation was not much better. Herman Rietzke remembered the first form of St. Paul mass transit as neither fast nor comfortable:

> At the Summit avenue hill the driver would hitch on an extra mule to get the passengers up the hill, but frequently it was necessary that a number of men would get out and not only walk, but help push the car up the incline. when on the hill the car ran to Nelson avenue [Marshall], and from Nelson the line extended to Western avenue, where there was a turntable. . . . Those old cars had neither heat nor light, in winter the bottom was covered with hay or straw, and on cold days all passengers would do the tread-mill act to keep their feet warm.

By 1880, St. Paul had grown quite slowly out to Dale Street, and residents of that western fringe of the city felt that they lived in the wilderness. The development of construction and city services had been retarded by the Civil War and the financial panic of 1873.

The Boom of the 1880s

With the opening of the new decade, however, St. Paul entered into a period of frenetic growth marked by wild real estate speculation, enormous civic boosterism,

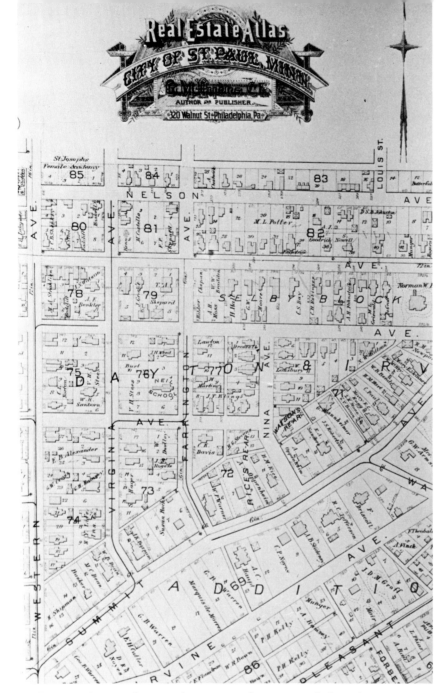

This model of the parlor organ was manufactured in North St. Paul in the 1890s.

Real estate atlases, such as Hopkins' 1885 edition pictured above, have proven useful in reconstructing the history of Summit Avenue.

The fifth house pictured on the dogsled photo, the Henry N. Paul house, stood at 294 Summit until 1919 (Bennett, Map of Ramsey County).

and greatly accelerated business and residential construction. The boom was probably the greatest in the history of the city. The St. Paul *Globe* reported in March 1882 that there had been only a moderate increase in real estate prices in 1881 but that the market was quickening. The extension of the city water system onto the bluff was promised "within a reasonable length of time" (*Globe*, May 7, 1882). On March 4 the next year the *Globe* announced that all of the property from Dale west to Macalester College, a distance of two miles, was now being sold by the foot instead of by the acre. "During the week all the lots unsold in the Palace addition fronting on the avenue were bought by one dealer and on the first of March all the lots in the addition were marked up from $50 to $100 per lot over preceding prices."

By 1886 annual real estate transfers in St. Paul amounted to $28,000,000, a sum which astounded even the most sanguine civic booster. The *Pioneer Press*, on January 1, 1887, took the trouble to look back to the beginning of the decade for the sake of comparison:

> In proportion to the size of the city, the real estate transfers of St. Paul for 1886 are the largest of any city in the United States. Such a record has never been surpassed by any city of 175,000 inhabitants. The question arises as to what are the details of this great deal of $28,000,000. The answer comes in the following comparative table of St. Paul transfers for five years:

Year	No. Transfers	Value
1882	4,447	$ 9,354,431
1883	4,847	12,981,381
1884	5,128	8,358,521
1885	6,822	14,318,687
1886	11,443	27,826,633
Total five years	32,687	$72,840,653

> The poor people — or what is called the middle class — have caused in part this stride forward. They have been heavy investors in the suburban resident property. The tables show this by the fact that the average transfer has not exceeded $3,000 in value. The number of transfers exceeding $100,000, or even $75,000, can almost be counted on the fingers. But

The Thurston house, 495 Summit, a splendidly preserved 1880s residence (Minnesota Historical Society).

the well-to-do artisans and mechanics who have been flocking into St. Paul for five years have been investing their savings in a site for a home. Then again the paving of Summit Avenue with asphalt and the proposed paving of other streets on St. Anthony Hill made resident property there very desirable. Crocus Hill property, two years ago practically inaccessible, now opened by graded streets, went up to $2,500 a lot.

Building on Summit Avenue reflected this rising tide of confidence and prosperity. In the five years 1882–1886, forty-six new houses were built, twenty-one of which still stand, and five of which were built west of Snelling Avenue. It was during these years that an especially noteworthy group of splendidly preserved houses between Arundel and Mackubin — 445, 465, 475, 476, 490, and 495 — were constructed. Although the

The brougham was a popular St. Paul summer vehicle (Minnesota Historical Society).

grandest and perhaps the best houses were not yet built, the construction of these five years established the character of Summit Avenue. By 1887 one historian of the city could proclaim:

> Summit Avenue is justly the city's pride. That magnificent street stands now without a rival in the West, with the single exception of Euclid Avenue in Cleveland. Following the edge of the lofty bluff which here looks down upon the city underneath, with the Mississippi winding its way from boundary to boundary, it is better fitted by nature for the handsomest residences that art can design and wealth construct than any other street in America. Its destiny is rapidly being fulfilled. Already the mansions of the moneyed men of St. Paul lift their imposing walls above its slopes of green. Each year sees added residences, surpassing all before them. Each year witnesses new plans for improvement and beautification. Paved with the smoothest of asphalt, preserving the undulations of its original design, and about to be widened and parked to the brink of the Mississippi, it will be one of the chief glories of St. Paul. It was less than two years ago that $150 per front foot was considered an extravagant price for property on the avenue. Last fall $350 per front foot was paid. Now no man could be so fortunate as to obtain a footing on the most desirable frontage at $500 per front foot.

The Horse on Summit Avenue

Although Summit Avenue's position on the bluff for its first mile contributed greatly to its character, there was something more to the avenue. Why, the twentieth-century observer wonders, why did the wealthy everywhere in Victorian America choose to build their houses along a single street — in the case of Summit Avenue, one more than four miles long? The answer can be found in the nature of the horse and the kind of

A bustle of horse-drawn traffic fills Summit Avenue in front of the James J. Hill mansion about 1890 (Northwest Magazine).

conspicuous consumption provided to the rich by horse-drawn vehicles. It is difficult for a generation which grew up with the democratic automobile to recognize that horses were particularly the playthings of the rich — not the draft horses which pulled the beer wagons and delivery vans, but the spirited trotting horses with their shining phaetons, broughams, surreys, and cabriolets for which the enormous carriage houses which line Maiden Lane were built. The ordinary citizen could not afford horses (which might easily cost more than $1,000 each), the expensive carriages, the hay and oats to feed the animals, and the stableboys and groomsmen necessary to care for them. Unlike an automobile, a good horse could not be locked up in a barn until needed but must be exercised every day. Taking the horses out for a drive became one of the most important social occasions of the day for a prosperous Victorian family. William Dean Howells, the American nineteenth-century novelist with

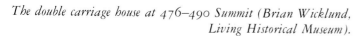

The double carriage house at 476–490 Summit (Brian Wicklund, Living Historical Museum).

An 1890s winter scene in front of 985 Summit (Living Historical Museum).

Children in a pony cart in front of 476 Summit in 1886 (Minnesota Historical Society).

Andrew Nippolt manufactured carriages like this in his shop on Sixth Street near Jackson in the 1890s.

the best sense of social history, described the role of the horse in terms which could just as easily have been applied to St. Paul instead of Boston:

> They met swiftly dashing sleighs, and let them pass on either hand, down the beautiful avenue narrowing with an admirably even sky-line in the perspective. They were not in a hurry. The mare jounced easily along, and they talked of the different houses on either side of the way. They had a crude taste in architecture, and they admired the worst. There were women's faces at many of the handsome windows, and once in a while a young man on the pavement caught his hat suddenly from his head, and bowed in response to some salutation from within. . . .
> The beautiful landscape widened to right and left of them, with the sunset redder and redder, over the low, irregular hills before them. They crossed the Milldam into Longwood; and here, from the crest of the first upland, stretched two endless lines, in which thousands of cutters went and came. . . . It was what [newspaper columnist] Bartley Hubbard called "a carnival of fashion and gaiety on the Brighton road," in his account of it. But most of the people in the elegant

sleighs and cutters had so little the air of the great world that one knowing it at all must have wondered where they and their money came from.

That was exactly what the people of St. Paul envisioned for Summit Avenue. Already by 1871 the residents of the avenue had paid to grade the street as far out as Dale, then the city limit. The *Pioneer Press* reported on August 9, 1871, "Before the summer is over it is expected that it will be much improved and rendered a very delightful and popular driveway." The word *driveway*, today a short pavement leading to a garage, then connoted a place of elegant promenade where one could see others and be seen. By the middle 1880s Summit had been paved, and, as Porter noted, was about to be "widened and parked."

Widening Summit Avenue

When Horace Cleveland, the landscape architect who eventually laid out Como Park and the Minneapolis park system, was paid $100 in 1872 to draw up plans for city improvement, the valuable bluff-side property was al-

Newly widened Summit Avenue shown in an 1890s photograph looking west from the roof of the Macalester College president's residence at Snelling and Summit (Macalester College archives).

ready built upon, and he was unable to create the kind of boulevard he would have liked. But by 1887 a group of property owners calling themselves the Summit Avenue Improvement Association had been organized to bring into existence a wide, park-like boulevard of the kind that was being popularized by Cleveland and his fellow landscape architects. The Association, led by Rush B. Wheeler, who at that time resided at 749 Summit, negotiated with all of the property owners from Lexington west to the river, a distance of two and a half miles, persuading them to donate enough land on each side of the street so that it could be widened from 100 to 200 feet, the land so obtained being placed into a central strip separating the driving lanes, planted with trees and shrubs, and furnished with a bridle path. Along this driveway the procession of carriages continued summer and winter until displaced by the automobile during the 1920s. In a real sense the disappearance of the horse marked, if not the end of the avenue, the end of its first great era.

CHAPTER 2

Preservation on Summit Avenue

Even on the best-preserved avenue in America, time takes its toll. Sixty-eight residences which once stood on Summit Avenue, about 15 per cent of the total number of houses built, have been demolished or moved. If there had been a historic preservation committee in nineteenth-century St. Paul, that group of citizens would already have had much to do on Summit Avenue by the 1880s, before most of the avenue had been built. As the Table of Razed and Moved Houses shows, from 1880 to 1960, an average of seven houses were torn down or moved off the avenue every decade; since 1960 only ten houses altogether have been razed or moved.

However, these statistics obscure a more significant fact. The character of the demolitions changed abruptly after the 1929 crash and the beginning of the Great Depression. With only seven exceptions, the houses razed before 1929 were replaced by new houses which in every case were more expensive, in most cases were better designed and more interesting than the houses they replaced, and which certainly added vigor and vitality to the avenue. Of the seven exceptions, three became the sites for Nathan Hale and Lookout parks, and two were cleared to make way for the Cathedral parking lot. Thus, until 1929 the process of demolition, even though quite extensive, cannot be viewed simply as a negative force but, rather, as part of a complex process of decay and further growth on the avenue. Landmarks such as the Neill house (242) and the Noyes house (366) were structures of real architectural and historic interest, but they were replaced by mansions of greater architectural and equal historic merit — the James J. Hill house (240) and the Boeckman house (366). Most of the other houses were structures of little significance.

During the 1930s, however, all seven of the houses which were torn down possessed high significance for the avenue and only one of them was replaced with a newer house. The other six properties remained vacant. In no other decade has the avenue suffered such an enormous loss. In the years following World War II, the process of demolition continued, but the razed houses were spread evenly over the length of the avenue diminishing the impact of their destruction. Furthermore, only five of the properties can properly be classified as vacant, and of these five only the lot at 555 Summit remains an obvious scar on the landscape, reminding one of the loss of the Rhodes house. (The other four are 378, 525, 755, and 854.) The greatest loss of the 1950s — and perhaps the

A fallen capital from the A. B. Stickney house, 288 Summit, symbolizes the fate of many fine residences in the 1930s (Brian Wicklund, Living Historical Museum).

15

Demolition on Summit Avenue:
Table of Razed and Moved Houses

Number of Houses by Address

Decade in which House Was Razed or Moved	1	2	3	4	5	6	7	8	9	10	11
1880–1889	226	236	242	252	251	266	288	410			
1890–1899	275	285	323	401	435	442	624	623	1620		
1900–1909	201	260	403	1034	345	301	857				
1910–1919	229	294	344	354	421	512	520	821	1017	1624	1093
1920–1929	217	236	366	1325	1127						
1930–1939	243	276	288	315	435	540	760				
1940–1949	545	1255									
1950–1959	226	378	779	1079	1494	1586	1596	2078	2106		
1960–1969	360	833	1035	1111	2064						
1970–	525	541	555	755	854						

entire history of the avenue — occurred in 1959, when the Amherst Wilder house (226) was torn down to make way for a new Archdiocesan Chancery.

Since 1960 the rate of demolition has dropped off sharply. The loss of the Cutler house (360) was much regretted, but restoration seemed prohibitively expensive at the time. Much less excusable was the destruction of the Hulehinge house (755) by the House of Hope Presbyterian Church. Except for these two instances, demolition has virtually ceased on historic Summit Avenue. Unfortunately, so has new building. Before analyzing the significance of this cycle, I shall provide short obituaries for the most memorable of the demolished houses on the avenue.

On the corner of Ramsey Street and Summit Avenue, on the site of the present Lookout Park, once stood a curious structure officially known as Summit Avenue House but described by most St. Paulites as Carpenter's Hotel or Carpenter's Lookout. The first structure on Summit to be demolished, it was also one of the few commercial buildings to be built on the Avenue (although the University Club directly across Ramsey Street seems to serve as a continuation of a tradition begun by Warren and Maria Carpenter). The hotel was built in 1859, or possibly in 1858, shortly after the Carpenters purchased that site as well as a large amount of land on the north side of Summit running across present-day Portland Avenue. As the picturesque sketch from 1892 makes clear, the hotel actually was built into the hill. Above the mansard roof on the fifth floor, patrons of the hotel can be seen taking in the vista from the balustraded captain's walk.

Maria died in 1872 and Warren in December 1886, and in 1887 as one of their first acts after their incorporation, the St. Paul Board of Park Commissioners took possession of the hotel site through condemnation proceedings. It has been a park since that date. Whether Carpenter's Lookout was demolished by the Park Board or had already been destroyed is not clear, but there is a local tradition that the hotel burned in the 1880s. The city did issue a building permit to Warren Carpenter a few months before his death for the construction of foundations for a larger structure than the one shown in the photographs and drawings. Since Carpenter died before the spring of 1887, when construction was scheduled to begin, it seems likely that the new building was never constructed and that the Park Board was taking possession of the property but not of the hotel itself. The fact that Carpenter's Lookout is not mentioned in the 1885 city directory lends further support to this line of argument. Carpenter's children continued to live on the remainder of the family property on the north side of the avenue and ran a hostelry at 403 Summit. By the turn of the century, however, this house along with 401 was also taken by the Park Board for Nathan Hale Park. There would seem to be some reason for supposing that the Park Board did not favor the operation of hotels on Summit Avenue.

An artist's sketch of the Carpenter Hotel, once located on the site of Lookout Park near Ramsey Hill (Northwest Magazine).

Among the other early houses demolished was the 1867 mansarded villa of Major Thomas Newson quaintly sketched by the traveling artist of the 1874 Andreas *Atlas*. Newson, an antiquarian and publisher, chose to describe himself in 1874 as an electrician, a puzzling statement for that era. This must refer to the fact that Newson was dabbling in healing by means of electric or galvanic shocks, for he also described himself as a "magnetic physician" in early city directories.

Only the front steps and some stonework at the rear of the lot remain of the twenty-two room mansion that once stood at 378 Summit. It was built in 1863 by Charles L. Emerson, publisher of the St. Paul *Democrat*. Other residents included the families of Albert McCarger, a cotton trader; J. P. Gribben, a lumber dealer; and Charles McIlrath, a grain merchant and state auditor from 1861 to 1873.

In the early 1890s, 378 Summit was purchased by Richards Gordon, co-founder of Gordon and Ferguson, a wholesale clothing and leather firm. The Gordons added a wing to the west side of the house in about 1908. Charles Gordon succeeded his father as owner of the house and president of Gordon and Ferguson, and his son, C. Richards Gordon, has recorded this recollection of his boyhood home:

It was a house of high ceilings, beautiful mahogany furniture and crystal chandeliers. Unfortunately, such things did not interest a boy. . . . What I

The best surviving photograph of Carpenter's Lookout (Minnesota Historical Society).

remember, above all, was the marvellous view of the bluff enjoyed from so many of the rooms, especially my mother's room which featured a series of windows in the southeast corner of the second floor. . . . The house was truly immense — a third floor where there were two big maids' rooms plus a great attic to explore; a second floor with five bedrooms, one dressing room, three bathrooms, plus a sleeping porch, facing the bluff, where my sister and I slept summer and winter (no matter how cold it was). The first floor contained the dining room and living room, both of which had fireplaces, a long drawing room, a breakfast room with windows on two sides, and a big pantry. The kitchen was located in the basement (a dumb waiter brought the food up to the pantry) as was the laundry room and a playroom equipped with a pool table and baskets for basketball. Below the basement was a cellar containing the furnace which made this a five story house.

The oldest known photograph of the house (1888) appears to predate any significant changes to the structure. Long-time Summit Avenue residents remember the house as a stucco-covered structure painted reddish brown. Its street facade seems to have been quite similar to 312 Summit; like that older house, the Emerson house was designed in the Italian villa style and sported the ornate window hoods which were fashionable in that period. The onion-domed round building to the right in the photo was a gardener's shed. At the time this house was demolished in 1957, no one could be found to rehabilitate and preserve the structure. Tearing it down was a pity, but not a decision that the historian can second guess.

The razing of the Cutler house at 360 Summit Avenue in 1968 was a similar case. Built in 1875, the house had

The A. B. Stickney and Rufus Jefferson houses at 288 and 276 Summit were both demolished in 1930 (Minnesota Historical Society).

been extensively remodelled in 1886 in such a way that by the mid-twentieth century the house had become structurally unsound and unattractive to potential occupants. When the house was torn down, doors, hardware, windows, and other decorative elements were preserved and incorporated into the attractively redesigned carriage house which can just be seen below street grade at the south edge of the property. The interest of the Cutler house for the architectural historian is the evidence it provides for nineteenth-century attitudes toward preservation. As can be seen in the photograph, the 1875 house was a large brick-veneered, two and a half story Tuscan villa with a three-story tower. The semi-mansard or curbed roof was covered with specially cut shingles. (It is interesting to note how unobscured the skyline beyond the house appears; apparently the bluff was not heavily

forested at that date.) By 1886 this house, although only ten years old, was no longer fashionable. Architects Willcox and Johnston added six feet to the east, west, and north sides of the house, and completely transformed the roof line. It is difficult to believe that two different houses are not pictured in these photographs. Careful detail-by-detail comparison, however, will reveal the basic similarity of the two buildings. What is worth comment, of course, is that the Cutler family, in typically nineteenth-century fashion, wanted an up-to-date looking house and had no interest in preserving the appearance of their Tuscan villa.

At 435 Summit Avenue there were two houses which preceded the present 1950s rambler. The site, directly across from the Burbank-Livingston-Griggs house, was built upon as early as the 1870s by W. A. Culbertson.

(Right) The Newson house at 236 Summit (Andreas Atlas). (Below) The Emerson house at 378 Summit, built in 1863 (Picturesque St. Paul).

An interesting photograph of this first house from the late 1880s shows the muddy track of Ramsey Street leading off to the right, and the open site on which the University Club would be built in 1912 in the immediate foreground. The Culbertson house (in the center) appears to have been a gabled and towered Italian or Tuscan villa of the type popular in the late 1870s in St. Paul. The cross-braced gable-end brackets are characteristic of the style. The stables can be seen to the right of the house, and on the extreme right-hand margin of the photo appears the Wheelock house (421 Summit), demolished in 1912. Behind the solitary figure in the middle of Summit Avenue rises the Shipman-Greve house (which still stands at 445) and beyond it the outline of the Constans house (455). When or why the Culbertson house was demolished is not known, but Michael Doran, one of the successful Irish residents on Summit Avenue, constructed the second house on the property in 1896 at a cost of $28,000, a great deal of money for a dwelling of that size. After the Dorans sold

Two versions of the same house. Above, the 1875 Tuscan villa-styled Cutler house at 360 Summit (courtesy Lucy Fricke). Left, the same house after remodelling in the Queen Anne style (Northwest Builder and Decorator).

21

Summit near the intersection with Ramsey Hill in 1888. From left to right, the residences at 465, 445, 435 (the Culbertson house), and 421 (the Wheelock house) (Minnesota Historical Society).

The Doran residence, 435 Summit, shown when it was the home of the Hibernian Club (Minnesota Historical Society).

the property, it was the residence of the George Slade family. The house was purportedly given to the Slades by James J. Hill, whose daughter Charlotte was the wife of George Slade. In the 1930s the house became the Hibernian Club. In the photo, an election poster for O'Connell can be seen hanging from the porch. In 1938 the house was wrecked, one of seven truly unfortunate losses for the avenue during the 1930s.

Two houses have also been demolished on the site of 226 Summit. The first of them was built in 1863 by George L. Otis, who served both as mayor of St. Paul and as a state senator. No records of the house have been preserved. The house was razed to make room for the Amherst Wilder house, built in 1887 at a cost of $77,000 and designed by Willcox and Johnston. Like his near neighbor James J. Hill, Wilder was involved in transportation development, first with stage and steamboat, then with railroads. His was certainly the grandest mansion of all the sixty-two which have been destroyed. Fortunately, a collection of excellent photographs help to preserve the memory of this splendid house. Built in the same year as Hill's mansion, and similarly classified as a Romanesque building, the Wilder house did not resemble the Hill house. Like other houses designed by Clarence Johnston — notably, 476 and 490 Summit built a few years earlier, and 587–601 Summit built two years later — the Wilder house reflects the work of an architect who has mastered the vocabulary of historic European styles, appears ready to enter a period of electicism, but has not lost his love of the massing and outlines of the late nineteenth-century picturesque styles, especially the Queen Anne.

Three houses on the avenue have been destroyed by fires — 275, 525, and 1111. The most disastrous fire in the early history of Summit Avenue occurred on February 8, 1895, at the Ansel Oppenheim residence at 275 Summit. Born in New York City, Oppenheim was vice president of the Chicago Midwest Railroad and one of the founders of the South St. Paul Union Stockyards. The blaze, which originated in the attic in an overheated chimney, totally destroyed the two and a half story, brick-veneered residence. The Oppenheims narrowly missed being destroyed themselves. A streetcar motorman returning home at 1:30 a.m. noticed the fire and alerted the family. Mr. and Mrs. Oppenheim, their three sons, and one servant dressed quickly and escaped from the house. Greve Oppenheim, one of the sons, must have been the last to leave the building, for as soon as he was down the steps, the staircase collapsed, sending up a shower of cinders and flames. The bitter cold drove the family into their barn, but they later joined the A. B. Stickney family across the street at 288 Summit for the remainder of the night. The morning revealed a completely gutted house and damage estimated by the fire department at nearly $18,000 to the house and $11,000 to the contents. The house was not rebuilt, and the family moved to the Aberdeen Hotel for the next fifteen years.

It is possibly more than a coincidence that none of the six houses built on Summit Avenue by architect Augustus F. Gauger has survived intact. The two at 295 and 465 have been considerably altered. The house at 301 was moved around the corner to 107 Farrington. The other three were demolished (243, 545, and 525), the last after fire broke out in the boarded house. Gauger was fond of the high tower, a favorite Victorian feature, which has not stood up to the challenge of time and Minnesota's harsh climate. None of his towers has survived even where the house itself has been preserved. The fate of these once fashionable towered residences illustrates a simple but often overlooked fact of historic pres-

The exterior and main parlor of the Amherst Wilder residence, 226 Summit, demolished in 1959 (Minnesota Historical Society).

1970 fire destroyed 525 Summit (Ariel Davidson).

Oppenheim house, 275 Summit, in 1895, after it was gutted by fire (Minnesota Historical Society).

ervation: not all buildings are equally easy to preserve. The fashion of the hour may dictate, as was true of the Queen Anne style, that the roof be steeply pitched, composed of many different planes, and characterized by numerous dormers and quaint overhangs. The roof looked good when new, but proved susceptible to leaking. In the 1920s cement tile was used on many roofs, especially houses of the Spanish Colonial Revival style. These roofs weathered well, but now are wearing out; many an owner is discovering not only that individual tiles are difficult to replace, but that the cost of removing the old tile and replacing it with some substitute is astonishingly expensive.

On a pleasant grassy spot between the Driscoll house (266) and the Lindsay-Weyerhaeuser house (294), there once stood two of the largest houses on the avenue, both begun in 1884, and both razed in 1930. The Rufus C. Jefferson house must have been virtually the twin of the Driscoll house on the next lot to the east, for both were built of brick and terra cotta with slate roofs, were de-

None of the towers so fancied by architect A. F. Gauger has survived. The Muir residence, 545 Summit, was demolished in 1944 (Picturesque St. Paul).

signed in the Queen Anne style, were constructed in 1884, cost about $25,000, and were of similar size and height. They were designed by different architects, of course, George Wirth being responsible for the Jefferson house.

The Stickney house (288) was a larger and more imposing, if not more attractive house. Designed by J. Walter Stevens at an estimated cost of $40,000, this immense Romanesque structure was occupied by only a single family, falling vacant after the first owner's death in 1916 and finally being razed in 1930 when no one could think of an appropriate tenant or alternative use. Such a waste seems even more incredible in view of the fact that each room on the first floor was finished in a different rare wood and that the ceiling of the reception hall was painted by the Swiss-born artist Carl Gutherz. Alpheus B. Stickney, the first and only owner of this mansion, was a red-bearded native of Maine who seems to have come to Minnesota at least in part for his health but remained to become the manager, superintendent, or

The A. B. Stickney house in 1888 (Picturesque St. Paul).

25

The Magoffin house, 344 Summit, demolished in 1914 (Picturesque St. Paul).

The Barnum house, 345 Summit, a quaint Tuscan villa set behind an attractive cast iron fence (Picturesque St. Paul).

president of five railroads; principal organizer of the South St. Paul Union Stockyards; and the inventor and builder of both a steam and a gasoline-powered automobile.

The Magoffin (344) and Barnum (345) houses were quaint and interesting structures, but had no real architectural distinction. George Wirth designed more attractive houses on the avenue than the one he built in 1886 for Samuel Magoffin; it was a modest residence on a relatively narrow lot. In 1904, the Barnum house was not razed but moved to Irvine Park, where it stood almost long enough to be included in that district's historic renewal. However, it burned in 1974 as a result of vandalism. The 1888 photograph shows the house as it must have looked when built in 1882. Its style represents a transition from the Italianate-Tuscan to the Queen Anne. The detailing of the porch, window treatment, bracketing and gable verge boards are all typically Italianate; the balconies, turrets, and expressive roof line seem to indicate the newer influences — though the curbed roof was never used with Queen Anne houses. The attractive and elaborate, probably cast-iron fence contributes to the villa-like or suburban effect which so many owners wanted to achieve.

A house of an entirely different level of architectural quality was the Daniel Noyes residence (366) built in 1884 for $20,000, designed by H. R. Marshall and the only example of that architect's work on Summit Avenue. Standing on the bluff high above the Mississippi, this house was the perfect St. Paul counterpart of the seaside villas being constructed in the 1880s at such summer resorts as Manchester-by-the-Sea or Newport by architects such as William Emerson, Eldon Deane, or McKim, Mead, and White. In contrast to the Magoffin and Barnum houses, both conservatively designed, the Noyes house was extraordinarily fashionable, even avant garde. This type of Queen Anne house is sometimes described as Shingle style, a name which derives from the common exterior covering of these houses, but which implies a new organization of interior space more than it does a kind of exterior decoration. Unfortunately, there is no surviving evidence about the floor plan of this house. Whether Marshall's quick adaptation of the new Eastern fashion went deeper than the walls, we cannot say.

The just-completed D. R. Noyes residence, 366 Summit, sparkles in this 1888 photograph (Picturesque St. Paul *).*

Any program for historic preservation on Summit Avenue should be based upon an understanding of the cycle of demolition reflected in the stories of these mansions. While the avenue was being constructed and leading citizens of the city were competing to erect their residences there, the chief danger to existing structures was produced by pressures of development — the possibility that someone with a great deal of money might be willing to demolish a perfectly sound, perhaps attractive older house in order to make a place for his own mansion. However, this has not happened since 1927. There was almost no new construction during the depression of the 1930s. The avenue lost its attraction for the rich after World War II when exclusive developments such as

North Oaks became popular, offering the same kind of woodsy, picturesque building sites which had been available on the bluffs on Summit Avenue in the 1880s. During the postwar decades, Summit Avenue was ·in great danger of disappearing, as have so many other fashionable boulevards when their moment of glory has passed. Almost by miracle, the houses survive. But this happy state can hardly continue without the development of a systematic preservation program. The property owners on Summit Avenue and all of St. Paul's citizens would be well advised in this decade to address the complicated but important questions of present use and future preservation.

27

CHAPTER 3

Zoning on Summit Avenue

The future preservation of Summit Avenue is closely related to the special zoning regulations controlling the street. As is true of the avenue in other respects, the history of zoning on Summit is unusual — and extremely complicated. Its intricacies remind one of diplomatic negotiations over the territories of Schleswig-Holstein. Lord Palmerston once quipped that only three men had ever fully understood the intricacies of the Schleswig-Holstein question and that unfortunately one of those men was dead, one had gone mad, and he himself, the third, had forgotten them. This chapter will attempt to rescue the question of Summit Avenue zoning from that fate.

Summit has always been predominantly a residential avenue. Yet, in the days before zoning regulations, a quaint mixture of business and commercial ventures were established on the street. Carpenter's Hotel, described in Chapter 2, was the earliest of these, followed by the University Club in 1912.

A simpler kind of food service must have been provided by the confectionary stand for which Mr. C. D. Chase took out a building permit in 1897. The stand was 14 × 36 feet, constructed of boards and tar paper at an estimated cost of $150 and located on the northwest corner of Summit and Snelling, across from Macalester College. The enterprising Mr. Chase may have expected that students would provide him with the bulk of his trade. But his tar paper shack, the first and only fast-food franchise on Summit Avenue, unlike McDonalds, did not prosper and soon disappeared.

Another unexpected use of Summit Avenue property occurred in 1890 when Messrs. Vogl and Puvogel took out a building permit to construct two greenhouses on the site of present-day 1017 Summit, across from the governor's mansion. Puvogel Florist is still a thriving business, though now moved a few blocks away to 949 Grand Avenue.

A gasoline filling station was planned, but apparently never constructed on the northwest corner of Summit and Kent. The Pure Oil Company intended to construct two one-story metal buildings on that site in 1914, but there is no evidence that they were ever erected.

Churches and colleges were an early feature of Summit's landscape, of course. Both Macalester College and the College of St. Thomas had been established in the nineteenth century, and by 1894 the St. Paul Seminary had separated from St. Thomas. By 1915 the new Cathedral of St. Paul, although not completed, had already

*Macalester College in the 1890s. In that day only faculty residences
fronted on Summit Avenue (Macalester College archives).*

been dedicated, and the First Church of Christ, Scientist;
the House of Hope Presbyterian Church; St. Paul's
Church on the Hill; and the Macalester Presbyterian
Church had all been built. No effort has ever been made
to prevent the building of schools and churches on the
avenue.

The construction of apartment houses did cause concern, however. By 1915 four sets of apartment buildings
had been constructed on Summit Avenue, all of them
within five years of the turn of the century: the first at
579 Summit (The Colonial) being built in 1895, two at
442 (The Livingston) and 550 Summit (The Oakland)
rising in 1898, and the last at 672–676 Summit (The
Waldorf) in 1900. When Summit was finally zoned to
single- and double-family occupancy, it had apparently
been the threat of more apartment buildings rather than

commercial development which stimulated the property
owners to seek the protection of the law. Residents of St.
Paul were aware that grand boulevards like Common-
wealth Avenue in Boston and Park Avenue in New York
had been transformed during the 1890s by the erection
of apartments. They were conservative enough to want to
retain the nineteenth-century character of Summit Avenue.

Zoning for the City of St. Paul, and for the whole of
the United States for that matter, was first imposed during the 1920s. Under the most recent revision of the
zoning code in October 1975, Summit Avenue was
zoned single-family residential. Unlike most of St. Paul's
streets, however, Summit Avenue land use is also governed by a special ordinance.

In 1915, in the era when zoning regulations were first

Johnston and Taylor were unsuccessful in this competition for the design of Macalester's Old Main (Macalester College archives).

being discussed nationally, the Minnesota state legislature passed a law (Ch. 128, 462.12 ff.) which stipulated:

> Any city of the first class [that is, Duluth, Minneapolis, or St. Paul] may, through its council, upon petition of fifty percent of the owners of the real estate in the district sought to be affected, designate . . . restricted residence districts.

The purpose of creating such districts was exactly the same as for modern zoning ordinances — the establishing of areas exclusively given over to single- or double-family housing. Restaurants, shops, factories, warehouses, coal yards, public garages, apartment houses, and flats were explicitly forbidden in the statutes. Some commentators have speculated that this 1915 law was actually a piece of special-interest legislation pushed through the legislature for the exclusive benefit of the residents of Summit Avenue. Such conjecture seems to be without foundation. The law was utilized widely in Minneapolis with almost a dozen districts being laid out, and it resulted in much adjudication in the courts. In one of these cases the City of Duluth filed a friend of the court brief indicating its interest in the legislation. Seven other restricted residence districts were projected in St. Paul in addition to the one along Summit Avenue, including districts on Mississippi River Boulevard, Marshall Avenue, Phalen Heights Park, and Cherokee Avenue. By 1922, in fact, the districts became so popular that St. Paul officials placed a moratorium upon creation of restricted districts while they worked on a city-wide zoning ordinance. The creation of these restricted residence districts within Minnesota played an

The Waldorf, 672–676 Summit, one of the apartment buildings which aroused interest in zoning regulations along Summit Avenue (Minnesota Historical Society).

important, but hitherto unappreciated part in the creation of city-wide zoning.

Procedures for implementing the 1915 statute were complex and time-consuming. First, 50 per cent of the property owners included within the boundaries of the projected district were required to sign a petition addressed to the city council. The original petition for Summit Avenue with signatures and indications of refusal remains in the vault of the St. Paul city clerk. The legal description of the boundaries of this district, when printed in the newspaper, overflowed to 232 lines, twenty-one column inches. It would have been simpler, if less precise, to state that the district included all property fronting on Summit Avenue between Selby and the River with the exception of the land on which the four apartments had been constructed. Also excluded was the property on the south side of Summit between Prior and Finn, where the residents chose to join another projected restricted residence district which included a good deal of Groveland Park.

Very few property owners refused to go along with the creation of the district, and many, through associations and clubs in which they held membership, made a special effort to lobby with the City Council for establishment of the district. Among those going on record in support of creating the district were the Woman's Civic League, the City Art Commission, the Woman's Welfare League, and the St. Paul Association of Commerce. All of these organizations, of course, included members who lived on Summit Avenue. In its letter of endorsement, the St. Paul Association of Commerce protested explicitly against the construction of an "apartment house building on Summit Avenue between Victoria and Oxford," making it apparent that the threat of additional apartment houses was the driving force behind the attempt to create the restricted residence district.

On August 4, 1916, the St. Paul City Council (File No. 11956) approved the establishment of the Summit Avenue district and on August 18 set in motion the next step in the process, appointment of a board of five assessors. This board was charged with determining which property owners would be damaged by the creation of this district and which would be benefited, charging a proportionate share of the damages to all of those who benefited. Or at least, that is what the law seems to indicate should have occurred. The assessors, following the guidelines laid down in the 1915 statute, mailed official notices of their first hearing, which took place on October 18, 1916; viewed the properties on the avenue; took testimony; and listened to objections. They filed their final report with the City Council late in the winter, and the City Council, over the protest of a number of property owners, accepted the report of the assessors and established the restricted residence district on April 7, 1917 (File No. 15762).

One can easily sympathize with the protesting property owners, because the procedures of the assessors and the action of the City Council appear perverse from almost any perspective. (The assessors' philosophy and methods were reported in great detail during the trial which followed the Council's action [District Court File No. 126640].) What seemed inexplicable to the protesting property owners was the assessors' refusal to acknowledge that any owners had suffered damages arising from the abrogation of their right to build apartment

The Manson house, 649 Summit, was converted into a funeral home in 1919 (Minnesota Historical Society).

buildings on their property. Instead, the assessors compensated owners of vacant land within 150 feet of all four nineteenth-century flat buildings. Their reasoning seems to have been that, since Summit Avenue was being restricted to single- and double-family occupancy, some compensation ought to be offered to those who would in the future be obliged to build dwellings next to one of the four existing apartments. In addition, a John McCarthy was offered damages of $4,500, by far the largest sum awarded, because the city attorney had advised the assessors that Mr. McCarthy's business, which occupied the rear of the property at 574 Summit Avenue (actually facing Oakland, but technically within the boundaries of the district), could not be improved or repaired in the future and was thus virtually condemned. For reasons which no one ever explained, the University Club, though within the district, was not treated as a commercial establishment.

Damages awarded by the assessors totaled $11,404. All property owners within the boundaries of the district were assessed relatively small amounts in order to raise this sum, the fees paid to the assessors, and other incidental expenses. These costs, apportioned according to property valuations, ranged from $5 to $50, with the majority of the owners paying less than $10 for the benefit of having their residence included within the district.

When, in spite of objections, the City Council approved the assessors' report on April 7, 1917, nine property owners filed suit to block the settlement and to obtain greater compensation. After the district court of Ramsey County in 1919 confirmed the action of the City Council, the plaintiffs appealed to the Minnesota Supreme Court. In its opinion in this case, *City of St. Paul v. Louis N. Scott and Others* (151 Minn. 115), the court upheld the validity of the city's actions, stating that the city had the right to draw the boundaries of a restricted residence district according to its own judgment. However, the court pointed out that the 1915 statute had contained a provision which allowed dissatisfied property owners to obtain a reassessment of their supposed damages by a second board of assessors appointed by the district court. Since the district court had not ordered this appeal and reassessment, the supreme court returned the case to the lower court.

On April 8, 1922, the district court of Ramsey County announced its judgment. The second board of assessors agreed that the plaintiffs, now reduced to five, had indeed suffered damages by having their right to build apartments on their vacant land nullified in the creation of the restricted residence district. The award of the court is summarized in the table that follows:

Plaintiff	Damages	Summit Address	Legal Description
Louis N. Scott	$ 6,112.20	850–854	Lots 13–14, Bl. 4 Summit Park Add.
Dickerman Investment Co.	4,912.20	720–722, 732–740	Lots 10–11 and 14–15, Bl. 6, Summit Park Add.
Arthur W. Drewry	$15,250.00	610–616	Lots 8–10, Bl. 4, Terrace Park Add.
John J. Watson and Anna C. Gibbs	8,500.00	456	The west 20′ of lot 2, all of lot 3, the east 50′ of lot 4, Summit Court rearr. of Terrace Court
C. H. F. Smith	5,400.00	556	The 90′ lying immed. east of the west 70′ of lot 6, Bl. 3, Terrace Park Add.

This award of more than $40,000 in damages would have created a much more significant charge for the other property owners on Summit Avenue and apparently produced consternation. Rather than pay the damages, the city attorneys worked out a compromise with at least three of the plaintiffs, Drewry, Watson and Gibbs, and Smith. According to this compromise, the city agreed to redraw the boundaries of the district so that these three blocks of land were left out of the district in the same manner as the four previously existing flat buildings. Thus, the property owners would suffer no infringement of their rights, and the rest of the Summit Avenue property owners would not have to pay their combined dam-

ages of nearly $30,000. Of course, neither would they be able to prevent the eventual construction of apartments on these plots. The St. Paul City Council passed a resolution formally exempting the Drewry, Watson-Gibbs, and Smith properties from inclusion in the new district on May 24, 1922 (File No. 39,801). The record is silent concerning the Scott and Dickerman properties, but, presumably their damages were paid and these properties remained within the district.

The Summit Avenue restricted residence district was thus finally established. In its final form, it included all property fronting on Summit Avenue between Selby and the Mississippi River except for those properties on the south side of Summit between Prior and Finn and the seven excluded parcels of land at 442, 456, 550, 556, 579, 610–616, and 672–676.

The Drewry property at the corner of Summit and Dale (610–616) was quickly developed. A large two-building complex containing fifty flats was constructed in 1927 at a cost of $140,000. The Watson and Gibbs land remained vacant until 1966, when a twenty-three-unit apartment complex was constructed by Strub and Associates. No structure of any kind has been built on Smith's property at 556, although the abandoned foundation for an apartment building begun in 1901 can still be seen in the underbrush.

During the same years that the case *City of St. Paul v. Scott* was testing the validity of the restricted residence district on Summit Avenue, the noncommercial character of the avenue was challenged in another way. On August 26, 1919, business partners John W. Kessler and Thomas S. Maguire purchased the residence at 649 Summit in order to establish a funeral home and mortuary on the premises. Since the property was included in the restricted residence district, neighbors might have challenged the validity of this action under the 1915 statute, but they chose instead to appeal to the St. Paul City Council, claiming the funeral home was a public nuisance. The City Council passed an ordinance on October 18, 1919, prohibiting location of funeral homes in residential neighborhoods. Kessler and Maguire were arrested for violating this ordinance when they began operation of their business. At the trial, newspapers gave a good deal of coverage to what they described as "sensational testimony" from such neighbors as Mr. John B. Meagler, Mrs. Everett Winter, Mrs. Rose Schurmeier, and Mrs. Charlotte Sanford. They testified that they were depressed and frightened by the presence of the funeral home in their neighborhood, that they were alarmed by the danger of disease being spread to their houses by flies, and that they were seriously thinking of moving. In a decision which technically upheld the right of the city to regulate the location of funeral homes in residential districts, Judge C. C. Haupt agreed with the protestors that "the concourse of mourning visitants and other insignia of mortality, tend to impair the peace, repose and health of surrounding residents."

This case also was appealed to the Minnesota Supreme Court, which upheld the district court. In the majority opinion in *City of St. Paul v. Kessler* (146 Minn. 124), Justice Andrew Holt argued that the 1915 state statute empowering St. Paul to establish restricted residential districts through the power of eminent domain, did not impair the police power previously vested in the city to prohibit certain businesses from locating where those businesses might become public nuisances.

On one more occasion the Summit Avenue restricted residence district came before the Minnesota Supreme Court. In this, the most famous of the Summit Avenue zoning disputes, the plaintiff was Warren Burger, presently Chief Justice of the United States Supreme Court, who in the 1950s was residing at 666 Summit Avenue. Coincidentally, this property was among those granted damages in the first assessors' report in 1917, and also, it is located almost directly across the street from 649 Summit, where Kessler and Maguire established their funeral home.

In 1943, apparently under the pressure of the wartime housing shortage, the Minnesota legislature amended the 1915 statute to allow owners of properties within restricted residential districts to convert their dwellings to fourplexes where the area enclosed by the foundation walls exceeded 1,000 square feet. No substantial alterations to the exterior of the buildings were permitted in the course of this remodeling. Many such conversions did take place uncontested in court. However, in 1951, Alvin J. Jansen applied for a permit to remodel 669 Summit into a fourplex, and after a hearing in which

One of the first automobiles on Summit Avenue, photographed in 1901 (Minnesota Historical Society).

(Left) The postman making his rounds on Holly Avenue in about 1890 (Minnesota Historical Society).
(Below) The intersection of Summit and Lexington in about 1925 (Minnesota Historical Society).

Warren Burger appeared to protest, Jansen was given City Council approval to proceed.

Burger sued the city to prevent his neighbor from altering his residence into a fourplex. *Burger v. St. Paul* (241 Minn. 285) was finally appealed to the Minnesota Supreme Court, which found in Burger's favor in 1954. The court ruled that the rights vested in property owners through the creation of the restricted residential district under the 1915 statute were themselves a property right which could not be taken away without compensation. The court therefore struck down the 1943 amendment to the law and reaffirmed the character of Summit Avenue as legally limited to single- and double-family occupancy.

In view of the extensive legal proceedings which have enveloped Summit Avenue and the great care which the courts have taken to protect its residential character, it must astonish anyone who walks down Summit in the middle 1970s to recognize virtually dozens of violations of this residential restriction within the first eight blocks. In 1975 the Summit Hill neighborhood association pressed St. Paul City officials to take some action in regard to these violations. This lobbying action resulted in a building department survey which revealed forty residences with more than two families residing on the premises, and six structures with ten or more apartments carved out of its rooms.

City officials have stated that they are reluctant to enforce the law because they feel that such action might be ruinous to present owners and possibly to the properties themselves. The spectre of vacant mansions moldering away with no buyer willing to accept their ownership certainly seems like a relic of the 1930s. Properties on Summit have been selling briskly in recent years, and prices for available houses have risen at least as fast as less historic dwellings. Meanwhile, buildings designed for single family residences are suffering the real dereliction that always accompanies the subdivision of such structures into one- and two-room apartments.

The conclusion of this chapter must repeat that of Chapter 2. No one in St. Paul has assumed responsibility for designing a long-range preservation plan for Summit Avenue. City officials charged with enforcing laws to protect the avenue refuse to carry out the clear intent of the law. Buildings which might yet be preserved as single-family residences are broken up into apartments or are used as cultural centers, schools, hospitality houses, churches, or office space — all uses which there is reason to believe the courts would find illegal under the 1915 statute since the buildings were originally constructed as residences.

If the restricted residence district imposes too severe limitations upon certain portions of the avenue during the 1970s, the law itself contains the relief of those grievances. The district was created by the property owners themselves. If they feel that some better plan for use of the avenue can be created and implemented, they can choose to lift the restrictions through the same process by which they were imposed. What seems tragic at this point in history is the assumption of helplessness and impotence which seems to grip property owners, city officials, neighborhood groups, and the general public. If the glory and beauty of Summit Avenue are ever lost, let no one fall back upon the feeble excuse that the dead hand of tradition and the complexities of an ancient law made preservation impossible.

Evening on Lower Summit Avenue (Leo A. Simmer, Minnesota Museum of Art).

38

CHAPTER 4

A Walking Tour of Summit Avenue

The best possible way to experience the architecture of Summit Avenue is on foot. This walking tour is designed to take one west from the Cathedral of St. Paul down the most famous mile on this historic boulevard. It is not possible to determine how long this tour will take since everything depends upon the willingness of the individual to stop in front of, photograph, sketch, discuss, admire, or criticize the houses. A brisk no-nonsense survey might require less than an hour for the walk down to Heather Place and back. A more leisurely schedule, which could include a thorough tour of the Cathedral, a visit to the Burbank-Livingston-Griggs house, and lunch or refreshments at the University Club or the Commodore Hotel, might occupy the whole of a very pleasant day. Many residents of the Twin Cities will want to divide the tour into smaller parts to match their own stamina and interests.

The tour begins with the site of the St. Paul Cathedral. A famous St. Paul pioneer first owned this land and built his brick homestead here around 1856. Jeremiah W. Selby is a familiar name in St. Paul since Selby Avenue, the southern boundary of this property, is named after him. Mr. Selby served variously as legislator, city assessor, and elder in the First Presbyterian Church. His widow, Stella, sold the property sometime after 1871 to Norman W. Kittson.

In 1882, Kittson built a huge Second Empire mansion on this hill. The architect was A. M. Radcliffe. Kittson had extensive real estate holdings, including a race track called Midway Park where Montgomery Ward now stands on University near Snelling Avenue. Kittson formed the Red River Transportation Co. with James J. Hill, had been a clerk for the Hudson Bay Company and a fur trader with Henry Sibley, and was once the mayor of St. Paul. His real estate and other business activities made him one of the wealthiest men in Minnesota. Kittson County in the northwest portion of the state is named after him. Kittson, a widower, died in 1888. In 1901 the "Kittson" became an elegant boarding house. It was razed in 1905 following its purchase by the Catholic Archdiocese in 1904 (see p. 77 for photo).

The Cathedral of St. Paul

This cathedral is a monument to the work of St. Paul's greatest churchman, Archbishop John Ireland. Ireland conceived of the grand scheme of this monumental building and was the key figure in the choice of the site, the

*Architect Emmanuel Masqueray's 1907 sketch of the east facade of the St. Paul Cathedral (*Western Architect*).*

selection of the architect, and the raising of the $1,500,000 eventually required to construct the edifice.

The architect was Emmanuel L. Masqueray, a Frenchman trained at the famous Ecole des Beaux Arts, where he won a number of prizes. He emigrated to the United States in the 1880s to work as a draftsman for Carrere and Hastings in New York. In 1903 he was chosen to be the chief designer of the St. Louis Louisiana Purchase Exposition, and it was in St. Louis that he and Ireland first met. Much of the work which Masqueray did for the St. Louis Exposition, especially the Festival Hall, bore a strong relationship to his later design for this cathedral.

Masqueray died in 1917 and Ireland in 1918. By that time the construction had been under way for over ten years, and the church was far from finished. The first mass had been celebrated in the unfinished building on Palm Sunday, March 28, 1915, amid the dust and confusion of ongoing construction. The heavy, granite bearing walls, the roof, and the dome were in place, but most of the interior finishing work remained for the future, and many of the windows were missing.

Archbishop Austin Dowling took over Ireland's responsibilities, and Whitney Warren became the architect. Warren designed the high altar and the baldachin (altar canopy). This work was completed by 1922; the rectory and sacristy were finished in 1925. In 1941 the last two of the great rose windows in the north and south transepts were placed in position, and the cathedral was complete.

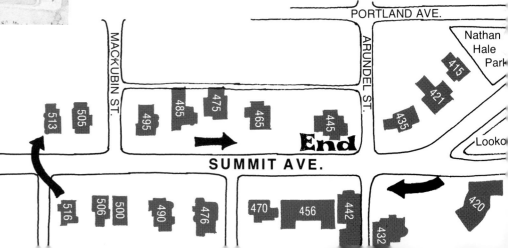

Masqueray's design of the cathedral was consciously modelled after St. Peter's in Rome. The grand dome, like that of Bramante and Michelangelo, is the key element, rising 306½ feet from the floor to the tip of the cross. The striking green of the roofing results from the natural weathering of the copper. The cathedral is normally open to visitors, who are urged, however, not to disturb anyone worshipping there.

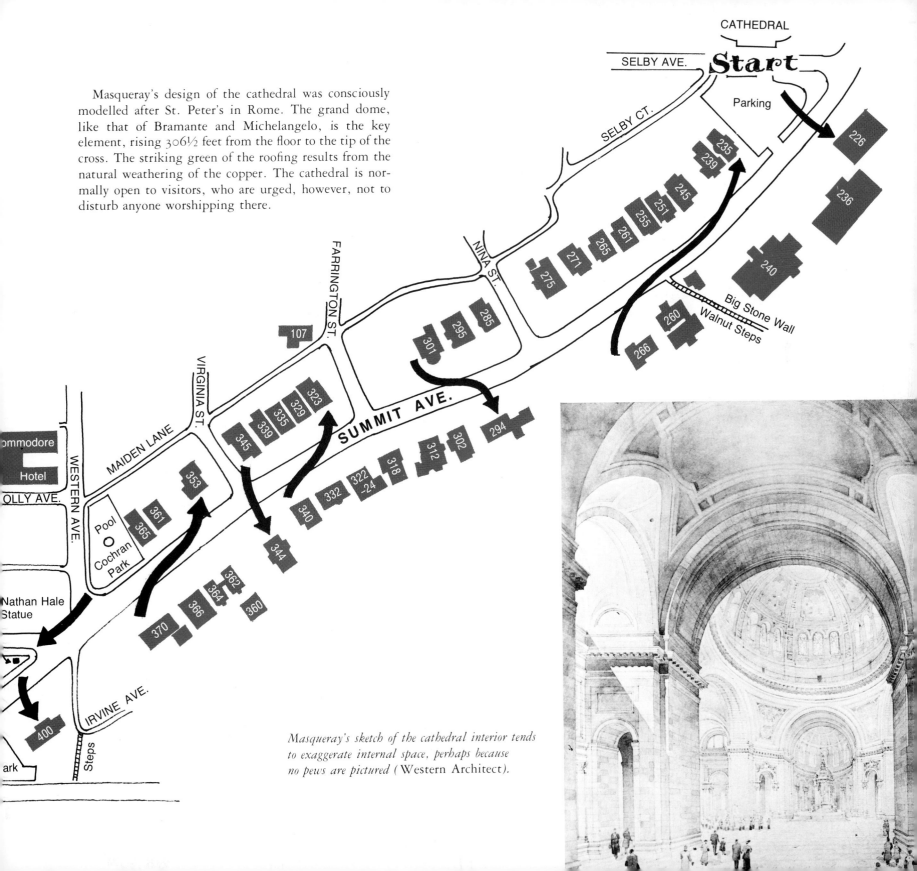

CATHEDRAL

Start

SELBY AVE.

Parking

SELBY CT.

226

235
239

236

245

251
255
261
265
271
275

240

Big Stone Wall

Walnut Steps

266
260

FARRINGTON ST.

NINA ST.

107

285
295
301

SUMMIT AVE.

VIRGINIA ST.

323
329
335
339
345

MAIDEN LANE

312
302
294

318
322-24
332
340

344

WESTERN AVE.

Commodore Hotel

OLLY AVE.

353
361
365

Pool
Cochran Park

Nathan Hale Statue

362
364
366
370

360

IRVINE AVE.

Steps

400

ark

Masqueray's sketch of the cathedral interior tends to exaggerate internal space, perhaps because no pews are pictured (Western Architect).

*Francis B. Clarke built this Queen Anne style residence at 236 Summit in 1882 (*Picturesque St. Paul*).*

226.　　On the bluff side of the Avenue, the two modern buildings house the Chancery Office of the Archdiocese and the Archbishop's residence. Both were designed by Cerny Associates and built in 1963. On the site of the Chancery, a lawyer prominent in early St. Paul purchased three lots in 1863 and built his house. Active in early city and state government, George L. Otis served as a state representative, state senator, and mayor of St. Paul. His house was razed in 1886 when Amherst H. Wilder acquired the property and built his mansion, designed by the architects Willcox and Johnston and costing about $77,000 (see p. 23 for photographs of the house). Wilder was a merchant, active in stage and steamboat transportation. Later in his career he was involved in railroading in Minnesota and adjoining states. The Wilder residence was purchased by the Catholic Archdiocese and served as the Archbishop's residence until the house was razed in 1959 to make way for the new Chancery.

236.　　On the site of Archbishop's residence (236) Thomas M. Newson lived from 1867 to 1879. We are indebted to Newson for his colorful short biographies of and anecdotes about the citizens of early St. Paul published in his book *Pen Pictures*. Newson was also a newspaperman and editor of the St. Paul *Times* (see p. 20 for a drawing of his house).

Francis B. Clarke acquired this property around 1882 and built a two-story frame dwelling, for an estimated $40,000. Clarke was general traffic manager for the Chicago, St. Paul, M. & O. Railway. This property was subsequently purchased by the Archdiocese of St. Paul, the house razed, and the new Chancery Office built in its place.

240.　　*The James J. Hill Mansion*
Continuing to the west, we come to the largest house on Summit Avenue, the James J. Hill mansion. A National Historic Landmark

since 1961, this 32-room mansion was designed by the Boston firm of Peabody and Stearns, and was built beginning in 1887 for an estimated cost of $280,000. The house contains 35 fireplaces, 18 bathrooms, a ballroom, a two-story art gallery with a skylight roof (on the east side of the house), and numerous parlors and bedrooms. The red sandstone exterior was designed in the Richardsonian Romanesque style with high chimneys, slate roof, and porte cochere with round arches. Spacious porches on the south give a view of downtown St. Paul and the Mississippi River.

The interior was lavishly decorated with carved and tiled fireplaces, ornate woodwork, and inlaid mosaics. A nine-foot-wide grand stair-

This view of the rear (south) facade of the Hill residence is not now visible because of the overgrown shrubbery (Minnesota Historical Society).

The monumental residence of James J. Hill, 240 Summit, begun in 1887 (Minnesota Historical Society).

The vestibule and grand staircase of the Hill house (Minnesota Historical Society).

case rises to a landing crowned by a wall of stained glass windows attributed to John Le Farge. Much of the woodwork is intricately carved, and inlaid marble is used profusely. The descendants of William Yungbauer, who was brought from Germany by Mr. Hill to do much of the woodcarving, are still cabinetmakers in St. Paul.

The large central hall stretches from the leather-covered walls of the dining room on the west to the sky-lighted gallery, complete with pipe organ, on the east. Opening off this hall are numerous smaller rooms, parlors, a breakfast room, James J. Hill's offices, an elevator, and doors to the porches on the south and east.

The second floor hall duplicates the first in size, with many bedroom suites and sitting rooms opening off it. More bedrooms and sitting rooms are located on the third floor; these were occupied by the children and servants of the household. A ballroom and children's playroom were built on the fourth floor. Since 1925, the mansion has been owned by the St. Paul Archdiocese, although in March, 1978, the State Historical Society seemed ready to conclude an agreement which would give them title to the property. The house is being restored and is now open to the public.

Much of the development of St. Paul and of the West as a whole was due to the efforts and vision of James J. Hill. Hill was essentially a railroad man interested in expanding railroad facilities and developing agriculture in the Northwest. Hill was born on a farm in Ontario, Canada, in 1838. At the age of 17 he came to St. Paul and was soon employed as a freight clerk in J. W. Bass's warehouse on the Mississippi River front. The goods destined for areas outside St. Paul were shipped by oxcart. This career in transportation, begun as a clerk on the levee, continued all his life until eventually Hill achieved his ultimate goal — a railroad across the Northwest to the Pacific Coast.

Hill numbered among his friends and business connections several well-remembered names in the early development of St. Paul. In 1869 he was in a fuel and transportation business with Chauncy W. Griggs; in 1870 he was active in the transportation of freight to the Red River Valley area, and this experience led to a partnership in 1872 with Norman Kittson in the Red River Valley Transportation Co. It was in 1878 that Hill succeeded in a business venture that would prove his genius in the transportation field. A railroad owned by Dutch interests was in serious financial trouble — the St. Paul and Pacific, with trackage from St. Paul to St. Anthony — and Hill had a great desire to acquire it. After many trips to Canada and meetings with friends there who shared his interest, he and several Canadians (including Norman Kittson) bought the railroad and reorganized it under the name of the St. Paul, Minneapolis, and Manitoba Railway Co. Hill was general manager until 1882 and became president in 1883.

William Yungbauer was the craftsman responsible for the exquisite woodcarving, such as these cherubs, found in the Hill mansion (Brian Wicklund, Living Historical Museum).

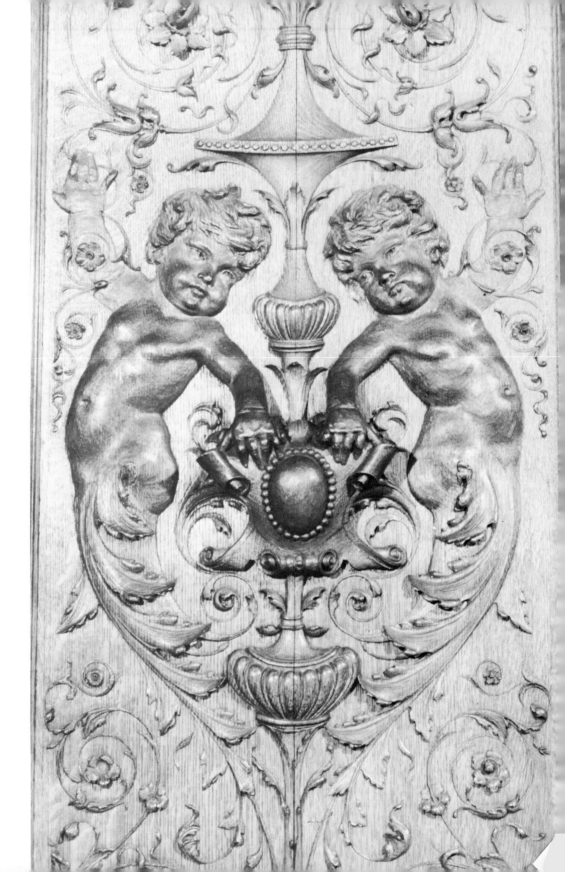

Rail lines were steadily expanded until they ultimately reached the Pacific coast. During this time the many small lines that had sprung up were acquired by Mr. Hill and added to the St. Paul and Pacific Railway, subsequently the Great Northern Railroad.

Two residences preceded the J. J. Hill house on this land. In 1855, Reverend Edward Duffield Neill lived at 242 Summit, in the house shown on p. 2. George W. Armstrong lived at 252 Summit Avenue from 1871 to 1885 in a frame house. He had come to St. Paul in 1853 and dealt in real estate and loans.

Two views of the Louis Hill residence, 260 Summit. Above, the house as completed in 1902 (Minnesota Historical Society). Below, as remodeled in 1912 (Living Historical Museum).

260.

Clarence Johnston designed this stately Beaux Arts Georgian mansion for Louis W. Hill, a son of James J. Hill. Construction began in 1902, and the estimated cost at that time was $40,000. The Louis Hill residence, despite its size, has all the charm of a gracious family home. It features a magnificent library with a massive fireplace intricately carved of Honduras mahogany, and a scrolled ceiling hand sculptured in plaster.

Across the large hallway, the banquet-size table and Chippendale chairs can accommodate thirty for dinner. Another large carved mahogany fireplace dominates the west wall; above it hangs a plaster copy of a Greek frieze, flanked by beautiful windows. French doors lead from the main hall to a solarium-breakfast room at the rear of the house which provides an excellent view of the city and river in the distance.

The front half of the house with its classical portico was added in 1912 and consists of four guest rooms with baths on the first floor and a beautiful ballroom covering almost the entire second floor. There is a full-size pipe organ, faced with wooden screens, at one end of the ballroom and a baronial fireplace at the other. There are few windows in this room, light being provided through a skylight of octagonal glass panes. The floor, like most of the flooring in the house, is parquet. The main kitchen was originally located

in the basement, food being brought by dumb waiter to a serving kitchen off the dining room. A swimming pool was also located in the basement, but this is now covered. The house is presently the Maryhill Retreat House.

266.   In 1884 this property was purchased by Frederick Driscoll, and the historic 1859 house on this property was razed to make way for the beautiful residence which William Willcox designed. Frederick Driscoll had a long and illustrious career in the newspaper business, which included many years as a partner with J. A. Wheelock in the St. Paul *Press* (which later merged with the *Pioneer*). In 1888, Driscoll built the Pioneer Press Building at Fourth and Robert streets.

Driscoll's red brick house is an excellent example of the Queen Anne style so popular in the 1880s, although it has been remodelled in ways which mute some of the characteristic features of that style. Still visible are the high-pitched roof with its many dormers and conical turret, pressed brick, and tall pilastered chimneys. The west bay is worth close attention, illustrating the Queen Anne picturesqueness most clearly: the chimney rises through all three stories, but the treatment of the windows is idiosyncratically different in each floor.

As the 1888 photograph of the house documents, the windows in the front stair tower, once stained glass, have been altered (probably in the twentieth century) to give the house a more neoclassical appearance. The new front portico was probably built at the same time.

Inside the house, the entrance hall has flooring of inlaid black-and-white marble squares and a white carved marble fireplace and mantel. The dining room has a stunning marble fireplace and wood mantel, heavily carved, with gilding and silver leaf. Silver leaf is used extensively in the woodwork trim all around the room. A sunroom has been added to the south of the long, gracious living room with a view down to the river.

Detail of woodcarving from the parlor overmantel in the Louis Hill house, 260 Summit (Brian Wicklund, Living Historical Museum).

The Driscoll house, 266 Summit. Above, the house as it appeared in 1888 (Picturesque St. Paul). Far right, the west gable and bay. Right, silver and gilt woodcarving from the dining room (Brian Wicklund, Living Historical Museum).

Frederick Driscoll moved to Chicago in 1900, and this house was purchased by Frederick Weyerhaeuser, a leader in the lumbering industry. Upon coming to St. Paul in 1891, Weyerhaeuser established headquarters for an ever-expanding timber-holding concern that reached to the Pacific Coast and was the largest company of its kind in the country. This house has been the headquarters for the Indianhead Council of the Boy Scouts of America, and is now the Epiphany House of Prayer.

On the open land to the west of the Driscoll house, there once stood two mansions built in the 1880s but razed in 1930. For pictures and discussion of the Jefferson and Stickney houses, see p. 19 and 24–25. Before continuing down the bluff side of Summit, let us retrace our steps to look at the first twelve houses on the north side of the avenue.

On the site of the present cathedral parking lot, there once stood two houses (217 and 229 Summit) of 1870s vintage which were razed about 1920 during the construction of the new cathedral.

235. Next to the parking lot stands a frame house built as a duplex in 1878 by Charles P. Noyes. From 1882 to 1896, the house was owned by Joseph McKey, who operated the Boston One-Price Clothing Store at Third and Robert streets. At present the house is being restored by new owners. An interesting, albeit unpretentious dwelling, it is one of the few surviving examples of a once common version of the Second Empire style.

239. William B. Bend, one-time secretary and treasurer of the St. Paul Harvester works, built

This 1888 photograph shows (left to right) the Hart house (243), now demolished; the Bend house (239); and the Noyes house (235) (Picturesque St. Paul).

this house in 1882 and lived here until 1908. In appearance, the house would seem to date from the 1920s owing to extensive remodeling. The house now serves as a nuns' residence.

The empty lot to the west was once the site of a residence built for Henry M. Hart in 1883, designed by A. F. Gauger at a cost of $11,000. James E. Moore lived here from 1889 to 1893. It is interesting to note that Moore was the chairman of the Summit Avenue Improvement Association which prepared the plans for widening Summit from Lexington to the river. Moore procured the written consent of the property owners to bear the expense of this improvement. This house was torn down about 1936.

245. Built in 1882 at an estimated cost of $10,000, this home was designed by the architect A. M. Radcliffe. The Charles Paul family originally owned the house and subsequently the Richards Gordons. In 1894 the George R. Finches acquired the property, and members of the Finch family lived here for over forty years. George Finch was a partner in an early wholesale firm in St. Paul which included, at one time or another, such well-known members of the business community as Maurice Auerbach, Joseph Forepaugh, and W. A. Culbertson, all Summit Avenue residents. Before George Finch died in 1910, the name of the firm was changed to Finch, Van Slyke, and McConville.

251. In 1866 Henry Morris owned this property, and he probably lived here until about 1875. In 1879 Horace P. Rugg is listed in the City Directory as living at this address, although the present large brick house was not built until 1887. The architects for this Romanesque style house were Hodgson and Stem, and the estimated cost to build it was $24,500. The design of the house seems to owe a considerable debt to Stanford White's Tiffany house, built in New York City in 1884.

Special features of the exterior of this building include carved stonework of classic nudes over the entrance arch, a peaked tile roof, and horizontal bands of dark-colored brick. A variety of woods was used throughout the structure — oak in the entrance hall and dining room, cherry in the living room, and sycamore and bird's-eye maple in the second-floor bedrooms. An interesting detail in the dining room is the Rugg monogram carved in the stone over the fireplace. Rugg's business was in wholesale pumps and railway and plumber's supplies. The building now houses the Catholic Education Center.

255–57. Unfortunately, this two-story brick double house of 1884 has suffered such serious delapidation over the years that its original design can barely be perceived. The two halves of the house were entirely separate, sharing only a common wall. The entrance to the former 257 can be seen on the west edge of the structure. In 1885, 255 was occupied by Lane K. Stone, a real estate broker; 257 was occupied by G. B. Bacon, an attorney.

261. Another house designed by Clarence Johnston, this gray-blue limestone residence was built in 1891 at a cost of $14,000. The first owners were the H. W. Kinney family and, a few years later, the family of James H. Weed, a pioneer St. Paul insurance man. The Weed family lived here for at least thirty-five years. Noteworthy details of the interior are the carvings and balustrades of the oak staircase. The neo-Gothic details on the house were most unusual in St. Paul in the early 1890s.

265. This red brick house was built in 1885 at a cost of $10,000, designed by C. W. Mould and first owned by J. S. Robertson. Distinguishing features are its fine octagonal tower and the carved stone medallion on the second floor.

The Horace Rugg residence, 251 Summit, was designed by Allen Stem in 1887 (North-west Builder and Decorator).

The Sanders house, 271 Summit, as it appeared in 1888 (Picturesque St. Paul).

F. A. Fogg built this house in 1899 after abandoning plans to rebuild Henry Rice's old house (Minnesota Historical Society).

271.   This was Joshua H. Sanders' house, built in 1882. Prominent St. Paul families living here through the years include those of E. W. Peet from 1887 to 1917 and R. B. Shepard from 1917 to 1928. Sanders was president of Northwestern Lime Co. As comparison with the photograph of 1888 shows, some changes have been made to the house, the most obvious of which is the remodeling of the front porch and the removal of the porte cochere. The central tower was restored in 1977.

275.   From 1880 to 1895 the house on this property was occupied by the Ansel Oppenheim family. A disastrous fire in 1895 caused the home to be razed (see p. 24 for a photograph).

By 1901 Charles Schuneman had purchased this land and built the house which stands here today. Mr. Schuneman was a prominent retail dry goods merchant and founder of a St. Paul department store which bore his name. C. H. Johnston was the architect of the buff-color limestone house, and the cost of building was about $18,000. During World War II, the twenty-five room house was divided into a dozen apartments. Today it is a reception house and private residence.

285.   In 1882, Henry M. Rice built on this property a two story wooden house with a mansard roof, costing about $6,500. This stood directly across the street from his 1850s residence pictured on p. 6. Henry Rice came to Fort Snelling in 1839 and was in charge of buying land from the Indians. About 1850 he bought a third of Dayton and Irvine's Addition for $1.50 an acre. Rice also owned eighty acres of land downtown where he built warehouses, hotels, and business blocks. He was a Congressman and a U.S. Senator. He lived at this address until 1894, when the property was acquired by Frederick A. Fogg.

F. A. Fogg was vice president of the Northwest Trust Co. and a director of the St. Paul Fire and Marine Insurance Co. In the late 1800s he served as superintendent of Ramsey County Schools and later as president of the Board of Education. In 1899, five years after he bought the house from Henry Rice, Fogg hired A. H. Stem to remodel the existing structure. But the building permit for general alterations was amended "on account of the building being new and not a alteration as intended," to quote the city clerk.

Stem designed an intriguing Rectilinear residence for the Foggs. Although the twentieth-century re-siding of the house disturbs what one hopes would have been a greater harmony among the design elements, the lovely giant order pilasters, the fan- and side-lit entrance, and other Georgian details are still worth comment. As you walk further down the avenue, recall this house when viewing another Stem residence at 340 Summit. A little farther away, at 30 Crocus Place in St. Paul, Stem designed a house in the same year as the Fogg residence which is virtually its twin save that the Crocus Place exterior is brick rather than wood.

295. Built in 1885 by Albert H. Lindeke at a cost of $13,000, and designed by the architect A. F. Gauger, this residence contains some beautiful woodwork — cherry paneling and trim in the two front parlors, with the dining room done entirely in bird's-eye maple. In 1903 a stone porch replaced the original wooden one, and some alterations were made inside by the architectural firm of Reed and Stem. The central entrance tower was probably removed at this time as well. An interesting feature of the front porch is the treatment of basement windows in the stone floor. These were originally covered with iron gratings, which have been replaced with glass brick.

Mr. Lindeke was one of the founders of the wholesale dry goods firm of Lindeke, Warner and Schurmeier, established in 1878. Albert W.

Two views of the A. H. Lindeke house, 295 Summit. Above, the house as it appears today. Left, the house in about 1900 (Souvenir of St. Paul).

The Gardner house, 301 Summit, now serves as a German cultural center (Brian Wicklund, Living Historical Museum).

Lindeke, his son, joined the firm and became a partner in 1903. He resided here with his parents and later built 345 Summit. The Society of Friends purchased this fourteen-room house in 1966 and uses it as their meetinghouse.

301.   In 1882, A. F. Gauger designed a frame house for this site at a cost of $7,500 for Dr. Alexander J. Stone, a physician and surgeon. About 1903 the house was moved around the corner to 107 Farrington where it still stands. By 1905 George W. Gardner had purchased the property and built the present Beaux Arts-inspired, Georgian stone mansion designed by Thomas Holyoke, at a cost of $28,000. Mr. Gardner was in real estate and insurance. This house remained in his family for many years. Today it is owned by the Volksfest Association of Minnesota.

315.   On the vacant site to the west of 301, architect James K. Taylor built a house for Mr. and Mrs. W. P. Warner in 1882 at an estimated cost of $12,000. The Warners' son, Richmond, continued living in the house with his own family until his death in 1936. Richmond Warner was treasurer of Griggs, Cooper and Co. The house was torn down in 1937.

Returning now to the bluff side of Summit, we will cross the street to view the white frame residence at 294.

294.   The first house which stood on this property is shown in the dogsled picture of 1859 and was owned by Henry Neill Paul (see p. 8). It was an Italian villa with bracketed eaves and a cupola. Subsequent owners were John Camp from 1870 to about 1880 and, later, Charles P. Noyes.

In 1919, George F. Lindsay erected the beautiful house which stands here today. He hired the Boston architectural firm of Parker, Thomas, and Rice to design his house; the cost was about

A wing has been added to the east end of the Lindsay house, 294 Summit, since it was constructed in 1919 (Minnesota Historical Society).

$30,000. Mr. Lindsay was associated with Frederick K. Weyerhaeuser in the lumber business. Lindsay lived here until 1932, when the house was purchased by the Weyerhaeusers; it has remained in that family for more than forty years.

302. In 1891 Joseph L. Forepaugh moved from his home at 276 South Exchange in Irvine Park (now a well-known restaurant) to this three-story brick house which had been designed for him by the architects Mould and McNicol, and was built in 1889 at a cost of $24,000. Forepaugh was a

member of the firm of Forepaugh and Tarbox, manufacturers and jobbers of boots and shoes. This house was owned by the Forepaugh family until 1947. It is presently divided into nineteen apartments.

312. Built in 1858 and pictured in the dogsled photo of 1859, this is the oldest house now standing on Summit Avenue. It was built for David Stuart in the Italian villa style. In 1918 a three-story addition was added, and some repairs were made to the house during the time that

An 1888 photograph of 312 Summit, the oldest house standing on the Avenue (Picturesque St. Paul).

Arthur Driscoll resided there. A front terrace with balustrade and a balustrade above the front door have been removed, but otherwise the facade has changed little throughout the years.

Several prominent St. Paul families have lived in this house, among them Brigadier General Herman Haupt, a graduate of West Point, an engineer in the Civil War, and the author of many scientific papers. It is believed that President Benjamin Harrison was entertained here by General Haupt. By 1882 Haupt had become general manager of the Northern Pacific Railroad. Another, later resident was Robert Armstrong Smith who came to St. Paul in 1853 as private secretary to his brother-in-law, Willis Gorman, territorial governor of Minnesota. Smith held many city and state offices in his career, including the office of mayor of St. Paul for several terms. The Arthur B. Driscoll family

owned this house from 1901 to 1949. Mr. Driscoll was the son of Frederick Driscoll (of 266 Summit) and was employed by the firm of Auerbach, Finch, and Culbertson; the St. Paul *Pioneer Press*; and the firm of McKibben, Driscoll, and Dorsey. At the present time the house is divided into several apartments.

318.   This Romanesque house designed by Cass Gilbert, was built in 1893. The rough-cut jasper and broad bands of darker brownstone give the house a massive, solid appearance. The deeply recessed second floor windows over the front entrance, as well as the strongly emphasized entrance arch, were design motifs which Gilbert repeated in later houses such as 505 Summit. It was built for a prominent St. Paul attorney, William H. Lightner, at a cost of $24,000 and was occupied by the Lightner family for over forty years. Further discussion and a photograph of the house are found on p. 82.

322–324. Law partners William H. Lightner and George B. Young built this double house in 1886. It was designed by Gilbert and Taylor and cost about $23,000 to build. The two residences were once completely independent save for their common central wall; they are now joined. The facade of the double house, although indicating the division between the two residences, nevertheless blends into a pleasing whole. Stonework on three floors of the Young residence at 324 contrasts with the stone on two floors of Lightner's beneath a gabled and shingled third story. The Romanesque arches of porches and windows also give continuity to the house. When his family outgrew this home at 322, Lightner built the house next door at 318.

*The Lightner-Young double house at 322–324 Summit (*Picturesque St. Paul*).*

332. Built in 1889 by Edgar Long, this home was designed by Gilbert and Taylor and cost $30,000. It has fourteen main rooms, a large entrance hall with fireplace, and a large hall on the second floor. It is distinguished by beautiful woodwork, much of it hand-carved, in oak, mahogany, and maple. Woodcarvings over the fireplace incorporate the date the house was built. The ceilings are of molded plaster fashioned in diamonds and circles, and the many fireplaces are constructed of different colored marble. The radiator covers are unusual in that they are made of cast iron to resemble tile or brick. The main floor rooms have parquet borders. The only exterior change made to this house has been conversion of the porte cochere to a kitchen with a garage underneath and a summer porch or storeroom above kitchen. The former kitchen was in the basement. Edgar Long was active in the lumber business and was general manager of the Railway Supply Co.

340. Designed by the St. Paul architectural firm of Reed and Stem in the style of an Italian Renaissance palace, this Beaux Arts residence was built in 1894 for Thomas B. Scott at a cost of $40,000.

*The east end of 332 Summit has been enclosed since this photo was taken (*Northwest Builder and Decorator*).*

This Beaux Arts influenced residence, 340 Summit, was designed by Allen Stem in 1894 (Souvenir of St. Paul).

Turning back to the north side of the street, we can see a group of five houses between Farrington and Virginia which stand close together on rather narrow sites.

323. A small stone house, built in 1863, first stood on this property — the home of John Roche, city comptroller for over twenty-one years.

Edward Nelson Saunders acquired the land in 1892. Clarence Johnston designed the present house for him at a cost of $35,000. The Romanesque porch arches are supported by columns with ornate capitals, each different. The front bay window also carries out this arched, sculptured effect. The house was occupied by the Saunders family until 1937 and presently serves as the Cathedral Convent (see p. 80 for an architect's sketch).

329. Built by Dr. Charles A. Wheaton, physician and surgeon, in 1895 and occupied by his family until 1913, this house cost $15,000 to build, but the architect is unknown. It bears a strong resemblance to the Rugg house at 251 Summit

in its powerful front gable flanked by brick chimneys and side entry with arched portico, but it is lighter in feeling.

335. J. H. Allen built this house in 1892 at a cost of $25,000. The architect was J. Walter Stevens. The house is constructed of Bayfield brownstone, but the rear third is red brick. Doric columns support the front porch. The entrance is enhanced by leaded glass sidelights. Prominent St. Paulites who lived here at one time were Joseph Stronge of Stronge-Warner Co. and Bernard Ridder, president of the St. Paul *Dispatch-Pioneer Press*.

339. Built in 1898 by Crawford Livingston at a cost of $14,000. The architect, Cass Gilbert, created an interesting effect in this house by bringing the second-floor facade forward over the customary front veranda, thus creating a kind of Italian loggia. The brick molding around the loggia arches and the diamond-shaped spandrel devices are also quite unusual. The Gothic-arched verge boards on the third story dormer do not seem to harmonize with the rest of the house, but they were

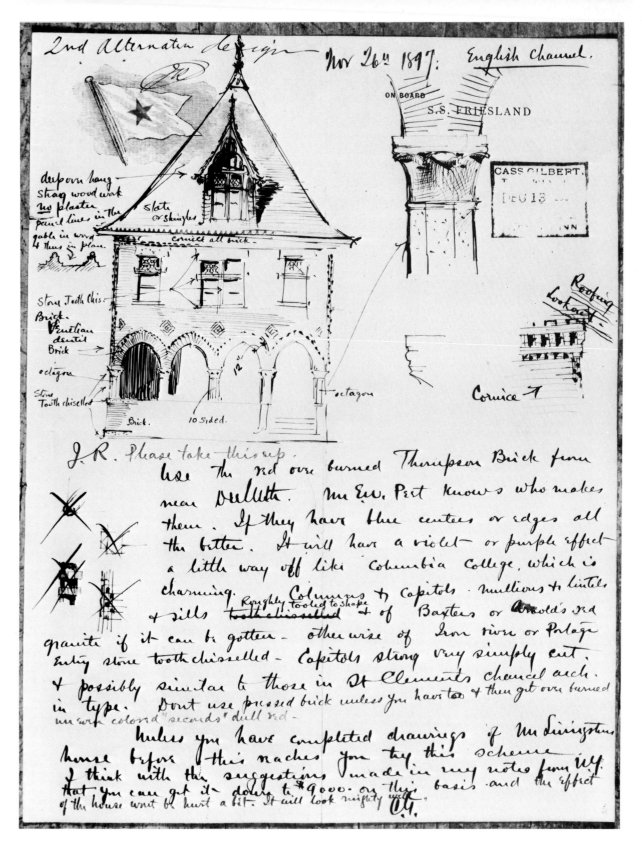

This Cass Gilbert letter contains his suggestions about the design of the Livingston house at 339 Summit (Minnesota Historical Society).

*The School of Associated Arts
now occupies the
Davidson house, 344 Summit,
an example of the reuse
of single-family dwellings
(Minnesota Historical Society).*

a favorite motif of Gilbert's: he used them again on the Dittenhofer house at 705 Summit. There, however, all the decorative devices are medieval, and the dormers seem more appropriate.

345.   A. K. Barnum, who worked in the real estate and loan business, built a large frame house with a central three story tower here in 1882 (see. p. 26 for a photo). About 1904 this house was moved to Irvine Park, where it stood until 1974, when it was razed.

In 1909 the present house was built by A. W. Lindeke, a partner with his father, A. H. Lindeke, in the wholesale dry goods firm of Lindeke, Warner, and Schurmeier. The A. W. Lindeke house was designed by C. H. Johnston and cost about $25,000. This was one of the first houses on Summit to be built in the Tudor villa style — with a brick first story, and second and third stories of stucco-and-beam construction. The brick wall surrounding the property matches the house and has an especially beautiful wrought-iron entrance gate.

Crossing the avenue again to the south side, we come to the present home of the School of the Associated Arts.

344.   A large stone house with a massive, two-story corner tower stood here in 1886, the property of Samuel M. Magoffin (photo on p. 26). Designed by the architect George Wirth, it cost $8,000 to build. When the property was purchased by Watson P. Davidson, Sr., in 1914, the house was torn down. In its place, the Davidsons built this Beaux Arts, Tudor manor house in 1915. Thomas Holyoke designed the house and it cost $40,000 to build. It has been occupied by the School of the Associated Arts since 1961. See p. 84 for further discussion and photograph.

360.   The E. H. Cutler family lived in a house built on this site in 1875. Cutler was a partner in the

Clarence Johnston designed this residence for the A. W. Lindeke family at 345 Summit (courtesy of Mary Proal Lindeke).

These condominiums at 362–364 Summit were built in 1977 and represent the first new construction on Lower Summit Avenue since 1954 (Living Historical Museum).

wholesale drug firm of Noyes Brothers and Cutler. (For photographs and description of this earlier house, see p. 18–21). Although that house was razed in 1968, the carriage house was converted to a dwelling by architect Joseph Michels, who integrated many parts of the old house into this remodeling.

The condominiums at 362–364 Summit, built in 1977, occupy the site of the Cutler residence. They are the first new construction on this portion of Summit Avenue since the 1950s. One might imagine that this evidence of the continued vitality of the avenue would have been greeted with cheers. Instead, the builder was involved in a controversy with neighborhood groups who contended that the design for the two buildings did not harmonize with the predominantly nineteenth-century character of Summit Avenue. However, as those who have walked this far down Summit Avenue can recognize, stylistic conformity is not the hallmark of

Summit — indeed, a great part of the historic value of the avenue lies in its reflection of the diversity of American architectural taste.

366.   Daniel R. Noyes, a partner in the wholesale drug firm of Noyes Brothers and Cutler which he helped found in 1868, built a residence here in 1884. (For photograph and description, see. p. 26–27.) This house was razed about 1924, when the property was purchased by Dr. Egil Boeckman, a prominent St. Paul physician. In 1928 he engaged the out-of-state architects David Adler and Robert Work to design the Georgian Revival mansion which stands here today. The estimated cost to build this house was $120,000. Interesting features include the eight chimneys topped with decorative cornices; the steeply pitched, curbed, slate roof; brick quoins on the corners of the house and garage; and the entrance pavillion, with its broken segmental arch. A striking feature of the first-floor vestibule

Last of the Hill family mansions and one of the best-designed houses on Summit Avenue;
the Boeckman house stands at 366 Summit (Minnesota Historical Society).

is its black-and-white marble floor with inlays of brass. The main floor rooms have beautiful parquet floors imported by Dr. Boeckman from a castle in Spain. Mrs. Boeckman was the former Rachel Hill, a daughter of James J. Hill.

370.   This is a Federal or Georgian Revival house designed by Clarence Johnston in 1909 for J. R. Mitchell. Its estimated cost was $15,000. Mitchell was president of the Capital National Bank of St. Paul and also of banks in Duluth and Winona.

.378.   A photograph and description of the house which once stood at 378 can be found on p. 17–20.

We will now retrace our steps for a few moments to look at the three houses on the north side of Summit between Virginia and Western.

353.   The house on this property was built in 1882 by William B. Dean at a cost of $15,000. Dean was a partner in Nicols, Dean, and Gregg, a wholesale hardware firm, and also served on the board of directors of the Great Northern Rail-

road. The house was remodeled sometime after 1900. A turn-of-the-century photograph shows that the dwelling was originally built in the Queen Anne style. The existing chimneys still reveal their stylistic origin.

361.   In 1882, C. S. Bunker built a two and one-half story frame house on this site. About 1912, the building was moved to 506 Summit, where it stands today. Donald S. Culver then built a new house at 361 in Tudor villa style. The architect was Peter J. Linhoff, and the cost was $12,000.

365.   In 1891 Mrs. J. W. Bass built a house on this property. Designed by James Knox Taylor, partner of Cass Gilbert, the house cost $20,000. Mrs. Bass, her son, and daughter-in-law exchanged houses in 1903 with the Chauncey M. Griggs family. It was Mr. Griggs who, sometime after 1903, added the striking, but inap-

The Dean house at 353 Summit has been greatly altered from its original Queen Anne style (Minnesota Historical Society).

In this wintry scene, the portico of the Bass house, 361 Summit, can be seen on the left (Minnesota Historical Society).

propriate Ionic portico to the front of this Queen Anne house

Cochran Park, the grassy triangle immediately west of 365, was deeded to the city on May 13, 1920, by Mrs. Thomas Cochran in memory of her husband, who had lived in St. Paul from 1869 to 1906. The Cochrans at one time owned a house across the street from the park on Western Avenue and also had resided in a house that once stood at 229 Summit.

To the north one block on Western Avenue stands the Commodore Hotel, once the residence of Scott and Zelda Fitzgerald. Although damaged by two severe explosions in March, 1978, the hotel is expected to reopen after renovation. The hotel bar is a stunning example of 1930s Art Deco design.

When you are ready to continue your tour, cross the avenue again in front of the statue of Nathan Hale to 400 Summit.

400. Built for Maurice and Matilda Rice Auerbach in 1882 by architect George Wirth, this three-story house was originally a Queen Anne style brick residence. In 1891 alterations extended the walls on the west and south sides of the house. It was probably during the 1920s, when the Lucius P. Ordways owned the house, that the Victorian facade was altered and the house remodeled to its present appearance. Maurice Auerbach, a son-in-law of Henry M. Rice, was active in early St. Paul dry goods firms, including Auerbach, Finch, and Culbertson in 1875 and Auerbach, Finch, and Van Slyke in 1881. He was also president of the Merchants National Bank and in 1860 had been a partner in the firm of Justice, Forepaugh, and Company. Later owners of this house were the W. P. Davidsons, Sr., 1913–1920, and the Lucius P. Ordways, 1923–1969.

In 1850 a portion of the eastern edge of this property was reserved as an extension of Western Avenue. In 1916 it was known as Petticoat Lane but now is marked simply "To Irvine."

The Auerbach house has undergone a startling transformation. Above, the house as it appeared in 1882; below, the house in 1977 (Living Historical Museum).

To the west of 400 lies the only section of the Summit Avenue bluff open to the public — Lookout Park, the first park created by the nineteenth-century St. Paul Park Board. This property was originally the site of a famous hotel, described on p. 16–17. After stopping for a few moments to enjoy the view, let us glance at the three houses across the street.

415.   An article in the St. Paul *Globe* on December 31, 1880, stated that William R. Marshall was building a two-story dwelling with a mansard roof at a cost of $8,500 on this property. It is not certain that Marshall ever lived in the house — in 1882, E. W. Winter, later president of the Northern Pacific Railroad, owned the property. In 1886 Winter built a $3,000 addition, and in 1907, William Dean made general repairs, including a new porch and bay window. It was possibly in 1907 that the beautiful Federal fan-lighted doorway was put in place.

421.   This house was built for E. T. Buxton in 1912 at a cost of about $22,500. It was designed by a Chicago-based architectural firm, Marshall and Fox. The Buxtons lived in this Beaux Arts Italian Renaissance residence for about eleven years. Dr. and Mrs. Egil Boeckman lived here from 1923 to 1930, when they moved into their new house at 366 Summit.

There had previously been another house on this property, built by J. A. Wheelock before 1882 (this house is pictured on p. 22). Wheelock had been editor of the *Pioneer Press* and a partner of Frederick Driscoll's.

435.   This modern brick rambler was built in 1954 by Chester Berry at a cost of $28,000. Photographs and descriptions of the two houses which previously stood on this site can be found on p. 22.

420.   The University Club stands on the bluff side of the avenue across Ramsey Street. This three-story brick and concrete clubhouse was built in 1913 at a cost of $100,000, and was designed by Reed and Stem. Although a private club, its bar and restaurant (from which there is a splendid view over the valley) is open to the public.

432.   The Burbank-Livingston-Griggs house was donated to the Minnesota Historical Society in 1968 by Mrs. Jackson Burke, who had inherited the house from her mother, Mrs. Theodore W. Griggs. This, the second-oldest house still standing on the avenue, was built by James Burbank in 1862 and was designed by Otis E. Wheelock of Chicago. Constructed of Mendota limestone, it was built in the Italian villa style, popular in the 1860s (see also p. 74).

Mr. Burbank was a highly successful entrepreneur, one of the foremost men in the transportation business in Minnesota, a partner with J. L. Merriam and A. H. Wilder in a wholesale grocery firm, a forwarding agent with the Hudson Bay Company, and in 1875 president of the St. Paul Fire & Marine Insurance Co.

Mr. Burbank's widow sold the house in 1884 to George R. Finch, a dry-goods merchant, who lived in it for about a year; he, in turn, sold it to Thomas F. Oakes, who later became president of the Northern Pacific Railroad. About 1889 Crawford Livingston, a successful banker and stockbroker, bought the mansion. His daughter, Mary, married Theodore Griggs (one of Chauncey W. Griggs's sons), and they occupied the house after the deaths of her parents. Mary Griggs remodeled the house extensively and added a new wing. Presently the house is closed.

442.   Summit Court Apartment House, built in 1898. The mansion of lumberman William Carson formerly stood on this site on a lot 250 feet wide and about 500 feet deep. Carson built his

The Burbank-Livingston-Griggs house as it appeared in the 1860s (Bennett, Map of Ramsey County).

brick house in 1876, and the Hopkins *Atlas* of 1885 shows that it was set well back on the lot west of James Burbank's.

456.   Colonial Apartments, built in 1966 by Strub and Associates. A twenty-three unit apartment house built on part of the old William Carson property. The zoning exception which allowed this apartment complex to be built on an avenue specially zoned for single- and double-family occupancy is explained in Chapter 3.

470.   This Spanish Colonial Revival tile-and-stucco house was designed by the architect Mark

The C. W. Griggs house at 476 Summit about 1900 (Souvenir of St. Paul).

Northwest, particularly in the Tacoma, Washington, area.

A fire in 1910 must have damaged the house considerably, because the estimated cost for restoring the structure was $18,000. Only $6,000 worth of repairs were made at that time; a subsequent owner hired a New York interior decorator to redesign the interior. The house was donated to the St. Paul Arts and Science Center in 1939 by Roger B. Shepard. At that time the front gable was removed and replaced by a skylight in order to bring north light into the painting studio. The original front porch has also been removed. The house is now a private residence.

490. This house was also designed by architect C. H. Johnston, in 1883 for A. G. Foster, a partner of Griggs in the lumber business. The three-story brick and wood structure cost about $23,000 and can be classified as a Romanesque building — although it is really only the round-arched windows which give it more of a Romanesque than a Queen Anne feeling. Johnston has used a great variety of design elements, including the prominent step gable which he used again at 1345–1347 Summit in 1900. Recent owners have altered the front porch and enclosed the third-story gallery, but otherwise the house is well preserved. A. G. Foster later became a United States Senator from Washington, having moved to Tacoma in 1887.

500. The red brick Georgian Revival residence of Dr. Cornelius Williams was built in 1904 at a cost of about $8,000. It was originally designed for a lot in lower town on the site of the present-day St. Paul Auditorium, according to a well-attested oral tradition. The Williams family decided that the lower town location was unsuitable and, instead, purchased the lot at 500 Summit, taking their house plans with them up the hill. The architect, Thomas Holyoke, was distressed over this move and wanted to design

Fitzpatrick, and was built in 1919 at an estimated cost of about $30,000 for the C. J. McConvilles. Mr. McConville was a partner in the dry goods firm of Finch, Van Slyke, and McConville.

476. This twenty-four-room stone house was built in 1883 by Chauncey W. Griggs. Architect C. H. Johnston designed it in the Romanesque style at a cost of about $35,000. An unusually large carriage house sited half on the Griggs property and half on the Foster property next door at 490, was constructed in 1882 at a cost of $12,000 (photo on p. 11). This building, also designed by C. H. Johnston, served as a workshop for the artisans constructing both the Griggs and Foster residences.

Chauncey W. Griggs is best remembered as the founder of the wholesale grocery house of Griggs, Cooper, and Co. He left St. Paul after 1887 and was responsible for the development of lumber and transportation businesses in the another house better suited to this lot, at that time part of an apple orchard. The Williams family, however, went ahead with their plans, placing their new house sideways on the lot with the main entrance facing east.

506. This house was originally built on the site of 361 Summit and was moved to 506 about 1912. The house must have been remodeled at that time by the new owners, C. W. and H. T. Talbert. Mr. and Mrs. Milton C. Lightner bought the house in 1923 and resided there until recently.

516. This Italian Renaissance Beaux Arts house was built in 1914 by William Butler in yellow brick with marble quoins, porches, and window surrounds, green tile roof, and deep bracketed eaves. Two windows and a set of French doors are grouped together under three arches on the Summit Avenue facade, the door leading to a marble terrace with a low balustrade.

William Butler was treasurer of the Butler Construction Co., the firm which built the State Capitol. The Butler family occupied this house for over thirty years, although purportedly they leased it for a short period to Sinclair Lewis, who in 1917 was working on a book about James J. Hill which he never completed.

This is as far as the walking tour progresses down the avenue. However, the interesting houses have by no means been exhausted. The index (p. 99) provides basic information on all of the houses, and you may, if you wish, follow that guide all the way to the Mississippi River. On this walking tour, we now cross to the north side of the avenue and walk back toward the Cathedral.

513. This attractively painted Queen Anne frame residence was built in 1891 at a cost of $10,000 for Mr. and Mrs. W. W. Bishop. No architect is listed on the building permit, so perhaps the

490 *Summit, built in 1883 for the A. G. Foster family* (Picturesque St. Paul).

475 *Summit, one of the few houses on Summit designed by George Wirth* (Picturesque St. Paul).

builder, John McDonald, drew up his own plans and specifications.

505. This Rectilinear Medieval-style house was designed by Cass Gilbert for George W. Freeman in 1896 at a cost of $20,000. The entrance and porch capitals are especially attractive, as are the verge boards in the dormer. Dr. and Mrs. Egil Boeckman lived in the house in 1917–1922.

495. Cyrus B. Thurston built this white-painted brick Queen Anne residence in 1881. The architect is not known. Originally, a small greenhouse stood on the east side of the first floor, but in 1967 it was converted into a patio.
In 1885 C. B. Thurston and Son was a business dealing in carriages and agricultural implements at 25 West Third Street. In 1891–1896, the family ran the Thurston Cold Storage and Warehouse Co. at 201 Eagle Street. Dr. and Mrs. Rudolph Shiffman lived at 495 about 1895–1905. A coat of arms including the initials R. S. was placed over the front steps when the Shiffmans resided in the house. Another photograph of 495 is found on p. 9.

485. This brick-and-timber Tudor villa was built in 1907 at a cost of $12,500 by J. A. MacLeod, who lived here for only a few years before selling to John G. Ordway. Members of the Ordway family occupied this house for over sixty years. In 1911 a two-story addition, designed by Reed and Stem, expanded the house. In 1922 a new sleeping porch and sunroom were added. J. G. Ordway, the son of Lucius P. Ordway, was an officer of the Crane Co. (formerly the Crane and Ordway Co.), manufacturers of plumbing and heating supplies.

475. Lumber dealer James Gamble built this Queen Anne house in 1883. Designed by George Wirth, it originally had a wooden porch with a lattice-work balustrade. In 1910, when the E. L. Hersey family owned the house, a $3,000 addi-

Cyrus Thurston placed one of the few date panels found on the avenue into the gable of 495 Summit (Brian Wicklund, Living Historical Museum).

tion was constructed on the west side of the house; presumably the porch was altered at that time as well.

465. In 1886, the architect A. F. Gauger designed this house for William Constans, French-born wholesale grocer and one-time partner of James Burbank in the commission business. The house itself cost about $18,400, and the carriage house $3,500. Thomas Newson in his *Pen Pictures* described Constans in 1886 as "the oldest continuous merchant in the City or State." Constans had in 1851 founded a wholesale firm dealing in hops, malts, and brewer's supplies. In 1883 this was the largest firm of its kind in the Northwest and the only one in St. Paul. Called Constans and Schmidt, it later evolved into the Schmidt Brewing Co.

The house was originally a Queen Anne mansion with a front porch and a five-story tower on the southeast corner. When Walter Hill occupied the house many years later, he removed the front porch and tower and added the Georgian moldings. It was again remodeled in 1968–1969.

445. Construction of this beautiful Queen Anne house was begun in 1882 by Henry Shipman. The architect is not known, but it is thought possibly to have been Leroy Buffington. Herman Greve, a real estate broker, acquired the house before it was completed. The Greves and, later, two of their married daughters and families — the George Kenyons and the Ansel Oppenheims — occupied the house until it was sold to Frank E. Ford in 1912. Ford added the low stone wall, iron fence, and the west wing, which includes a den and sleeping porch. In 1925 Mrs. Arnold Kalman (Sarah Greve) bought back her father's house, and members of her family owned it until 1950. The house is noted for its beautiful interior woodwork and Japanese-inspired lattice work visible on the porch. For further description of this house, see p. 79.

The William Constans house at 465 Summit (Minnesota Historical Society).

The Shipman-Greve residence, 445 Summit, photographed before the addition of the west wing (Minnesota Historical Society).

A brass drawer pull from the dining room sideboard in the James J. Hill residence (Brian Wicklund, Living Historical Museum).

CHAPTER 5

The Styles and Architects of Summit Avenue

Looking at old houses has become a favorite American pastime, a recreation akin to bird watching. As ornithologists have provided field guides to the many species of American birds, this chapter will attempt to provide an introduction to architectural style. As the comparison with bird watching suggests, the house watcher must be aware of the possibility of finding local variations in house styles as he or she travels from area to area. There are birds whose range is limited to a few small islands; there are also house styles which have flourished in quite restricted locations. The Prairie style, for example, was seldom popular outside the hinterland of Chicago. Students of architectural history are sometimes confused and frustrated in attempts to apply guidebooks on architectural style, usually written from the perspective of New York or Chicago, to what they see in their own towns, not appreciating the fact that the process of understanding must proceed in the other direction — inductively, from the individual house to a description of the general type. Summit Avenue provides an ideal sample with which to conduct such an inductive study.

St. Paul developed a distinct architectural style in the generation preceding World War I. American architec-

tural history during that period has been focused upon the great figures of Sullivan, Wright, and the Prairie School. There has been a tendency to neglect other, local traditions or to assume that what did not conform or adapt itself to the canons of the new architecture must have been devoid of merit and integrity. In this chapter we shall look at a few of the excellent houses which were built on the avenue in each era of its history. In addition, I hope to show that Summit Avenue architecture from 1890 to 1910 represented a different but equally authentic response to the same problems being confronted by the Prairie School.

The Picturesque

During the nineteenth century, Summit Avenue architecture reflected national stylistic trends quite faithfully. Until the 1890s, new architectural fads swept across the country in waves, each new style supplanting its predecessor and being supplanted by its successor. In contrast to the Georgian and Classical Revival buildings of the eighteenth and early nineteenth centuries, which were restrained, controlled, and rational in design, most middle and late nineteenth-century houses expressed the

The Burbank-Livingston-Griggs house (Brian Wicklund, Living Historical Museum).

feeling of the picturesque. Not a style in itself, the picturesque is, rather, a point of view through which all the arts in the nineteenth century passed on their way to romanticism. In architecture, the last of the arts to feel the impact of the picturesque, buildings were designed to emphasize such qualities as roughness, intricacy, sudden variation, and abruptness. As in the paintings of the Hudson River School, an attempt was made to surprise or startle the subject. The house was designed with the intention of confronting the eye, rather than the mind — to make a visual impact. And again in contrast to the classical approach, the house was supposed to fit into its natural setting, to be viewed as a part of the landscape and to give its owners "views" — perhaps startling or breath-taking views framed by its windows, porches, and balconies.

The Burbank-Livingston-Griggs House

The Civil War mansion of James C. Burbank at 432 Summit is a superb example of the Italian villa style and an embodiment of the picturesque. Of the five Italianate houses constructed on the bluff only two remain. The Burbank-Livingston-Griggs house, although greatly altered, retains the essential elements of its setting, outline, and ambiance. It is the queen of Summit Avenue.

The Italian villa style was characterized by round-headed windows, a low-pitched roof (often topped with a cupola), and eaves decorated by brackets — all distinctive features of the Burbank house. Unfortunately, the verandas of the Burbank house have all been altered or removed. Instead of decorative hoods or window moldings (customary in Italian villas), quoin blocks entirely outline the windows of the first and second floor.

Nothing is known about the architect of this house, Otis E. Wheelock, save that he was reputedly a Chicagoan.

Tuscan and Second Empire Styles

Following the Civil War, the Italianate style gradually evolved into the Tuscan and Second Empire styles. No examples of the Tuscan style survive on Summit Avenue, but the now-demolished Cutler house (p. 21) illustrates the mode. It is distinguished from the Italianate by its lofty entrance tower.

The Second Empire style, named after the imperial regime of Napoleon III, was really only Italianate with a new roof line, the mansard. Named after its originator, seventeenth-century French architect François Marsart, this roof style was revived by the enlargement of the Louvre in 1852–1857. The 1874 Manson house at 649 Summit (p. 33) illustrates a vernacular version of the Second Empire style, but the Ramsey house is St. Paul's best high-style version of Second Empire.

Vernacular Styles

During the 1870s and 1880s two other vernacular or local styles were built in St. Paul in great numbers and are represented on Summit by eight examples; four of these survive, and early photographs of six of them help us to verify their original appearance. The four Macalester College faculty residences at 1586, 1596, 1620, and 1624 Summit and the Jackson house at 1722 Summit resembled one another closely. (The Jackson house is perhaps the only nineteenth-century house on Summit Avenue in which the family of the original owner still resides.) Simplicity and restraint were the common features of these houses. Only in the strapwork applique in the gables, the use of shingles, the simple bays, and the single round window do we recognize gestures toward high style. I have categorized them as Vernacular Stick style. Houses like these are seldom represented in guidebooks, and since they possess so little pretension to style (although they are attractive), it may not be strictly proper to attempt to categorize them. Their existence points up the fact that not every variety of American architecture is pictured in the style books.

The Noyes house at 235 Summit (p. 49) and the Stone house (moved to Farrington from 301 Summit) also defy standard stylistic categories. Again, there are many contemporary examples of this house style in the Historic Hill District — at 454 Ashland and at 557 and 563 Dayton, for example. These houses are characterized by a curbed roof, cross-braced and hooded gables, pierced-work verge boards, and subdued eaves brackets.

Vernacular houses of the 1880s. Above, 1624 Summit, a Macalester College faculty residence. Below, 1722 Summit, the Jackson house (Macalester College archives).

The curbed roof, actually a high-pitched hip roof cut off before it reaches its peak, is often mistaken for a mansard. However, since the mansard is a disguised additional story, it is always pierced with many dormers. This is not true of the curbed roof. Nevertheless, these houses may represent a local adaptation or vernacular imitation of Second Empire; for this reason I have described 235 and 301 Summit as Vernacular — Second Empire. Since all of these are frame dwellings, it may also be true that this is a particular adaptation of the basic Italianate-Second Empire tradition rendered in wood.

These picturesque variations of the villa styles — Italianate, Tuscan, and Second Empire — represented the total vocabulary of styles on Summit Avenue down through the 1870s. As noted in Chapter 1, a building boom hit St. Paul in general and Summit Avenue in particular during the early 1880s. This boom coincided in the history of St. Paul with a change in architectural taste and an influx of new architectural talent.

The Architectural Old Guard

The old guard was made up of architects such as A. M. Radcliffe and Edward P. Bassford. Radcliffe (1827–1886) was one of the earliest of Minnesota's architects, setting up his practice in Minneapolis before Minnesota became a state and establishing his office in St. Paul in 1858. Two of Radcliffe's Summit Avenue houses still stand (245 and 534), but they are both completely altered, their original style now indistinguishable. We do know that the houses he built for Norman W. Kittson at 201 Summit and for Henry M. Rice at 285 Summit in 1882 were both designed in the Second Empire style. Edward P. Bassford, a leading St. Paul architect during this era, designed only a single house on Summit, 1093 in 1891.

George Wirth, a St. Paul architect with a large Midwestern practice which included commissions in Hastings, Duluth, and the Dakotas, was younger than Radcliffe and Bassford, but his prolific and important work on Summit Avenue is limited to the years 1882–1886. The Bend (239) and Auerbach (400) houses have been completely altered, and the Jefferson (276) and Magoffin (344) houses demolished, but the Bunker house (built at 361 but moved to 506) and the Gamble house (475) (p. 69) still exist. Although the Gamble house is attractive, most of Wirth's other work appears to have been quite conventional.

Herman Kretz and Augustus F. Gauger were both German-born architects. Kretz (1860–1931) was also trained in Germany. Although Kretz built a great deal, he specialized in commercial and apartment construction, owning and managing many of the buildings he designed. Gauger (1852–1931) came to the United States as a boy of ten, learned carpentry, and then apprenticed as an architect. When he came to St. Paul in 1875, he worked in the office of E. P. Bassford before setting up his own practice. Since he was a practicing architect well into the twentieth century, it seems significant that Gauger's six commissions on Summit were limited to the years 1882–1886 and were usually designed in a florid, late 1870s Second Empire or Tuscan villa style. They must have seemed old fashioned to the bright young men with whom Gauger worked in Bassford's office.

The New Architects

The phalanx of new talent that captured most of the prize commissions in the next few decades were strikingly similar in background. Clarence Johnston (1859–1936), Cass Gilbert (1859–1934), James Knox Taylor (1857–1929), Allen Stem (1856–1931), and J. Walter Stevens (1857–1937) were born within a year or two of one another, were reared in St. Paul, and in their early twenties were ready to practice just at the moment that the great building boom hit St. Paul. Close friends, Johnston, Gilbert, and Taylor, studied together in Boston at the new school of architecture at the Massachusetts Institute of Technology. They had all apprenticed in Radcliffe's or Bassford's offices before leaving for M.I.T. Johnston returned to St. Paul after one year at M.I.T. and began to work as a draftsman for Bassford. By 1882 he had opened his own office. Gilbert finished the two year course at M.I.T., traveled in Europe for a year (Johnston did the same in the winter of 1882–1883), and then joined the well-known New York firm of McKim,

The mansard roofed, Second Empire style mansion of Norman Kittson stood on the site of the St. Paul Cathedral (Minnesota Historical Society).

Mead, and White. He returned to St. Paul to set up practice late in 1882, shortly after establishing a partnership with James K. Taylor which lasted until 1892, when Taylor left St. Paul to become the architect for the U.S. Treasury Department. One of the draftsmen in the Gilbert and Taylor office was Thomas Holyoke (1866–1925), who had been educated at Harvard and *atelier* Duray in Paris. Holyoke opened his own office in the 1890s.

These new architects never monopolized building in St. Paul, and, during the 1880s, when they were still in their early twenties, it seems remarkable that they were able to win any commissions at all. However, a battle between new and old styles, between young and old designers was taking place. In America in the 1880s, it is not surprising to discover that the new and the young were victorious.

The Queen Anne Style

The new style was called the Queen Anne, although some historians have used synonyms such as Tory style. The style originated in England, popularized particularly by Richard Norman Shaw, a British architect who specialized in rambling mansions which resembled the seventeenth-century manor houses of the aristocracy. The American public saw several Queen Anne style buildings at the 1876 Philadelphia Centennial Exposition, where houses designed in this new mode were built as a part of the British exhibit. Henry H. Richardson designed a Queen Anne house in 1874 at Newport, Rhode Island; the Watts Sherman house excited a great deal of interest among architects.

In contrast to the Italianate styles, the roof of the Queen Anne house was high-pitched and peaked, its planes interrupted as often as possible by dormers, gables, and turrets. The outline of the walls was equally varied, with bays, towers, porches, and balconies breaking up the surface of every wall. Many different kinds of building materials were used: stone, brick, wood, shingles, slate, and half-timbering frequently being found upon the same house. Stained glass was popular, as were leaded glass and casement windows. The style was, in short, the epitome of the picturesque.

The Shipman-Greve House

The Shipman-Greve House at 445 Summit is a perfect example of the Queen Anne style, its attractiveness enhanced by the fact that it is beautifully preserved. The only change has been the addition of a two story porch on the west side of the house in 1912. Almost a textbook illustration of the style, the Shipman-Greve house is built of limestone up to the second floor, the second floor is sheathed in wood and plaster half-timbering, and the third floor gable ends are covered in a wavy-patterned slate. The pilastered chimneys are brick. The roof line is more subdued than some Queen Annes, but still exhibits three different levels as well as a shed roof over the porch for contrast. The porch, a part of the house which frequently is replaced without much thought for authenticity, has been perfectly preserved. The Japanese-inspired design of the lattice work is another bequest of the Philadelphia Centennial, where Japanese art first made a large-scale impact on American connoisseurs. Many Queen Anne houses were fitted with this same type of decoration.

The architect of this masterpiece is not known. Nothing else resembling it was constructed in St. Paul, so it is not possible to attribute the house through stylistic similarities to someone known to be practicing in the city. A family tradition has linked the house with Leroy Buffington, the Minneapolis architect, but this is weak evidence for even a tentative attribution. Whoever designed the house was not only a master architect but also one thoroughly familiar with the latest developments. That two German immigrant families — the Shipmans, who began the construction, and the Greves, who completed it — should have chosen to design such an avant-garde Anglo-American house is certainly worthy of comment, even though we may not fully understand the reasons for their choice.

The Battle of Styles

The battle of styles ended quickly. The first Queen Anne design, the attractive house at 495 Summit (p. 9 and 70), appeared in 1881. By 1883 only Augustus Gauger was designing Italianate houses, the last of which

The most perfect Queen Anne house on the avenue, the Shipman-Greve house, 445 Summit (Minnesota Historical Society).

Clarence Johnston's pencil sketch of his design for the E. N. Saunders house, 323 Summit (Minnesota Historical Society).

was erected at 545 Summit in 1886. The Queen Anne style dominated the construction of the 1880s on Summit Avenue. By the middle 1880s, Wirth, Radcliffe, and Gauger had won their last commissions, and the names of Gilbert and Taylor, Stem, and Johnston had begun to dominate the list — preeminently the name of Clarence H. Johnston.

It is ironic that we know so little about Clarence Johnston, for he was probably the most important single figure in the history of architecture in Minnesota. Gilbert, Stem, and Taylor all left the state or worked outside the state on commissions which have gained them national reputations. But Johnston stayed home. He built virtually the whole of the pre-World War II University of Minnesota campus, many state hospitals and prisons, as well as a great many commercial buildings. And he designed thirty-five houses on Summit Avenue, thirty-five of the finest houses.

Two of Johnston's earliest commissions on Summit Avenue, the C. W. Griggs house at 476 and the A. G. Foster house next door to the west at 490 Summit, have remained favorites of St. Paul natives and visitors alike (see p. 68–69 for photographs). That Johnston, not yet twenty-five, should have won this double commission from two important and influential families speaks well of his talent and reputation, but probably also says something about the social circle in which his family moved. He was not a stranger to St. Paul. That Johnston designed 476, the more impressive of the two houses, is not conclusively established. The two houses were constructed simultaneously, however, with their common barn (p. 11) used as a construction workshop. Johnston did design 490, and the similarity of the design of 476 to the later, Amherst Wilder house leads one to believe that he worked on both houses.

The Romanesque Style

They are important houses in the history of Summit Avenue because they represent the first use of the Romanesque style, a mode in which Johnston designed some of his finest houses. Romanesque, like Queen Anne, was a nostalgic style, turning to early medieval architecture for some of its design motifs. Also like

Queen Anne, it was a style made up of bits and pieces of historic structures, with an attempt to recapture the feeling (again that picturesque phrase) of the Middle Ages, but without any desire to recreate entire Romanesque buildings. Romanesque is essentially a style for building in stone, occasionally in brick (as in 490 or 323 Summit), never in wood. When the architect does not use stone, the style tends to wander toward Queen Anne and the distinctions between the styles begin to merge.

In the bold use of masonry construction the Romanesque finds its truest expression. More massive than the Queen Anne, the Romanesque was frequently used for commercial buildings, hotels, warehouses, railroad stations. Its popularity for residences was not very great in the United States. It seems significant, then, that Romanesque houses appear quite frequently on Summit, thirteen of them being built during the 1880s and 1890s in comparison with twenty-four Queen Annes.

The great Boston architect, Henry Hobson Richardson, popularized the Romanesque style. No one has ever built in masonry with greater effectiveness than Richardson, and his many famous commissions in the Boston area must have been visited by Johnston and Gilbert on their regular sketching trips. Trinity Church, Boston, was built in 1873–1877, just before Taylor, Gilbert, and Johnston matriculated at M.I.T. Sever Hall, Harvard University, was being built while they were students.

The best-known Romanesque house on Summit Avenue is the James J. Hill mansion designed by the Boston firm of Peabody and Stearns. Although impressive and large enough to suit anyone's notion of baronial splendor, the house is not really attractive. The Hill mansion illustrates the danger of Romanesque — that the massive qualities of the construction may create forbidding images of castles or (worse) warehouses, rather than the inviting and friendly vision of the rural villa. The late nineteenth-century city *was* becoming a more dangerous place in which to live, and many architects, including Frank Lloyd Wright, designed houses which isolated and protected their clients from a hostile environment. But it was possible to use the Romanesque style in ways which emphasized the strength and protection afforded by the dwelling, without losing delicacy or projecting hostility.

Above, the Lightner house, 318 Summit (Living Historical Museum). Below, Cass Gilbert's caricature of himself as a travelling artist (Minnesota Historical Society).

"This sketch is quite a successful failure, is it not?"

"OUR special Artist" veiwing the Promised Land.

The Lightner House at 318 Summit

Cass Gilbert succeeded in building such a house for the Lightner family at 318 Summit. This house uniformly wins the approval and admiration of groups touring Summit Avenue. The influence of H. H. Richardson upon Gilbert's design of the house must be obvious to any student of Richardson's work. The large blocks of rough-surfaced Sioux Falls jasper contrasting with the accents and belt course of Bayfield brownstone remind one of Richardson's use of masonry in Trinity Church or in the Crane Memorial Public Library in Quincy, Massachusetts. The arch over the entrance is so much a Richardson trademark that it is usually called the Richardson arch. But Richardson never built a house which looks like the Lightner house. Gilbert here created something quite distinctive. What most impresses the sidewalk admirer is the compactness and unity of the design. Gilbert, like some of the best modern architects, reduced the essence of a style to a single, balanced, eloquent declaration. The design is expressed clearly, succinctly, with nothing left over. And the house is not intimidating: the architect has successfully escaped the trap of building a warehouse and calling it a mansion.

From Italian villa to Romanesque, the styles we have been describing followed one another like floats in a parade. The appearance of a new style demanded the disappearance of the old. During the 1890s this pattern broke down. New styles appeared but the older ones refused to go away. There is, thus, no one style being built at a given moment during the twentieth century as was true during the nineteenth. This architectural pluralism certainly reflects profound changes in American society. There is some reason to feel that this stylistic diversity was a symptom of the fragmenting of American culture, but it is perhaps more reasonable to argue that at this point in history Americans desired greater variety in the appearance of their houses.

The Beaux Arts Tradition

The stylistic tradition known at the Beaux Arts illustrates this thirst for variety. The name Beaux Arts derives ultimately from the architectural school of the French State, the Ecole des Beaux Arts (School of Fine

Arts). Richard Morris Hunt attended the Ecole in 1846, the first of a large number of American students to seek training there. When professional architectural schools were established in the United States, they consciously imitated the curriculum and methods of the Ecole. This was certainly the case at M.I.T. where Johnston, Gilbert, and Taylor studied.

In France, the Beaux Arts tradition — stretching back to the seventeenth century — meant the centralized control of architectural taste, concentration upon the classical tradition, emphasis upon careful drawing and rendering of building designs as much as actual construction, and a grand scale in those buildings which were constructed. Much of this was impossible in America; the impact of the Beaux Arts tradition upon Americans was limited by the conditions of our society. The turn-of-the-century work of McKim, Mead, and White (especially the designs of Stanford White) epitomize the Beaux Arts style in the United States. The Columbian Exposition of 1893 in Chicago reflected the triumph of the style.

The young men who took over leadership in St. Paul architecture during the 1880s were all disciples of the Beaux Arts tradition. Cass Gilbert had apprenticed with Stanford White. His draftsman, Thomas Holyoke, had worked in a Parisian architect's office (atelier) connected with the Ecole des Beaux Arts. The best-known public buildings by each of them was in the Beaux Art style — New York's Grand Central Station for Allen Stem; Northrop Auditorium at the University of Minnesota for Clarence Johnston; and the Minnesota State Capitol for Gilbert.

When building a private residence, Beaux Arts-trained architects were forced to adapt their style to the limits of their patrons' building site, budget, and taste. Under these restrictions, one surviving aspect of their Beaux Arts training was a deeply cultivated sense of history. These architects had been trained to understand and appreciate the grand tradition of European architecture in a way which, ironically, even European-born architects like Kretz and Gauger failed to do.

Every American style had, of course, been derived from Europe. The Italian villa, Queen Anne, and Romanesque were all ways of adapting European material to American needs. But the Beaux Arts architect treated this material differently. First, because of the emphasis upon the sketching of buildings in their professional training, they began to "see" the buildings in their environment in a way that only the artist is capable of grasping. Gilbert's correspondence from M.I.T. reveals that he was spending several hours each day traveling to sites in the vicinity of Boston to sketch roof rafters, a rood screen, or an attractive facade. Many of their assignments at M.I.T. involved submitting drawings of perhaps a bridge or bell tower which would then be judged, critiqued before the class, and, in Gilbert and Johnston's cases, brought home to be framed and hung on their walls. The capstone of Gilbert's career at M.I.T. seems to have been his winning second prize in an important drawing competition.

When architects trained in this manner were turned loose on a European tour, they went out as traveling artists. Gilbert even facetiously drew a sketch of himself as a traveling artist for Johnston's amusement. On his long European tour, Gilbert became an expert in the cost of paper and sketching supplies. And when Johnston planned a four-month trip in 1883, Gilbert gave him extensive advice on his itinerary, concluding, "the places I mention are the ones [where] you will find stuff of immediate use to you." Clearly these trips were not holidays so much as mining or harvesting expeditions. Into their sketchbooks went hundreds of drawings which would later appear as elements of houses on Summit Avenue. As they sketched, they also were able to perceive these buildings as wholes, grasping the essence of their design and gaining an appreciation of the whole sweep of European design from ancient Greece and Rome through the Middle Ages to the Renaissance. This experience gave them a freedom previously unavailable to American artists. In the act of viewing this architecture as history, they also distanced themselves from it. They realized that the Europeans had created a grand variety of expressive forms which they as Americans were free to use wherever they felt those styles produced the right effect. Classic; medieval; Italian, Dutch, and English Renaissance — all these styles were sketched and filed in the architect's sketchbook and memory, waiting for a client whose need they met.

The Beaux Arts tradition was exactly what St. Paul's leading citizens seemed to want at the turn of the century. During the twenty years of building following 1890, virtually every house built might be described as belonging to the Beaux Arts tradition. St. Paul was emerging as the queen city of the Northwest, challenged by bumptious Minneapolis to be sure, but without question the center of culture for this region. The St. Paul residents who chose to live on Summit Avenue wished to live in houses which reflected this turn-of-the-century notion of culture.

The most popular form of Beaux Arts house was the small-scale version of the Italian Renaissance palace. There are six examples of the Italian *palazzo* on Summit, the best of them being Stem's version at 340 Summit and the impressive brick residence at 808 Summit designed by Green and Wicks of Buffalo, New York. The Dutch Renaissance double house at 1345–1347, designed by Clarence Johnston, possesses probably the most picturesque silhouette on Summit. One can imagine Johnston finding elements of that facade in his sketchbook.

The Davidson House at 344 Summit

The Davidson House, designed by Thomas G. Holyoke, captures the character of the Beaux Arts at its best. The design is derived from the late-sixteenth-century English manor houses of the Midlands, and Holyoke has captured the essence of that tradition perfectly. At the Lightner house, Cass Gilbert built in the Romanesque style, but that house does not evoke recollections of any particular building in Europe. Elements of the design are drawn from the tradition of Romanesque architecture, but the design of the building as a

The Davidson House, 344 Summit (Brian Wicklund, Living Historical Museum).

84

*Three examples of Clarence Johnston's design interests. Above and right,
drawings from his sketchbook. Top right, 1345–1347 Summit, built for Walter
and Pierce Butler in 1900 (Minnesota Historical Society).*

whole is completely fresh. In the Davidson house, Holyoke is not using design elements but adapting and reforming the idea of a Tudor manor house. He did not copy any particular house, but recreated in St. Paul a living embodiment of that form. Leaving aside for the moment the question of whether any architect ought to attempt that feat, let us first recognize that it represents a considerable degree of skill and imagination. Holyoke obviously mastered the intricacies of this style and reproduced the window hoods, entrance arch, and chimneys with fidelity to the Tudor precedent. But he then combined them into a comprehensive design which itself expressed that same fidelity — a task demanding more imagination that most critics will concede.

During most of the twentieth century, the Beaux Arts tradition has had a bad press. Beaux Arts designs have been faulted because they were not sufficiently functional, because they did not express American tastes and needs, and because they were too woodenly dependent upon models drawn from an aristocratic tradition. At its worst (and, of course, any style is subject to degradation), the Beaux Arts could deteriorate into supplying fake castles for counterfeit noblemen; the designs sometimes did lack taste, amounting to little more than an assemblage of spare parts for a chateau. Or at another extreme, a passion for things European could lead an enthusiast like Mary L. Griggs to import entire rooms from abroad to refurbish the mansion at 432 Summit.

But no art historian should judge a style by its aberrations, but rather by its successes. It is my judgment that Summit Avenue contains some excellent examples of the Beaux Arts tradition. These houses continue to impress the public and hold the affection of their owners not only because they look like a Tudor mansion or an Italian *palazzo*, but also because in looking like their European counterparts they give expression to a sense of history and (why not?) Romanticism which is otherwise neglected in the United States, and because they evoke these feelings with a use of space and decoration which sustains their owners in a way that pure functionalism seldom has. It seems ironic to recognize that it is exactly these qualities which have given a worldwide reputation to the best houses of Sullivan and Wright.

The Georgian Revival Style

The Beaux Arts style generated one form of retrospective design that is probably the best-known and most-copied design in the United States. This style is usually called Georgian Revival. The basic Georgian Revival house is constructed of brick, its main block a rectangle sited long side to the front, its symmetrical facade marked by a center entrance flanked by an equal number of windows on each side. There is a sprinkling of houses which I have labeled Georgian Revival dating earlier than 1910, but the style definitely rose in popularity on Summit Avenue in the second decade of the century. Over fifty houses were eventually constructed in this style, the red brick, traditional version remaining popular through the 1920s. However, a version of the Georgian Revival which I have called Early Modern Georgian Revival does appear at about the same time. This house is stripped of applied decoration (pilasters, urns, swags), is finished in stucco, and bears the same wide eaves as Early Modern Rectilinear houses. The same cravings which make Beaux Arts European revivals popular seem also to feed the desire for Georgian Revival dwellings. The coincidence of their popularity with the Progressive Era emphasizes those strains of nostalgia for the early virtues of America which historians have shown to be prominent in the politics of that period.

The Rectilinear Style

Of all the stylistic categories used in classifying houses on Summit Avenue, by far the largest number of houses has been placed in the group known as Rectilinear. The name will puzzle many readers because there is nothing known as the Rectilinear style to be found in most guidebooks. Hasbruck and Sprague in *A Survey of Historic Architecture of the Village of Oak Park, Illinois* (1974) are the first to use this term, to my knowledge — finding it necessary in order to classify all of Oak Park's residences. As has been my experience in working on Summit Avenue, they found that many houses do not fit the mostly nineteenth-century stylistic types found in the textbooks.

In surveying Summit Avenue, I have noticed that a subtle change begins to affect houses in the middle 1890s. With no other stylistic alteration, the basic shape of the house begins to alter, moving away from the irregular outline so characteristic of the picturesque styles toward a basic rectilinear shape. In contrast to the Georgian Revival house, which is, of course, also basically rectilinear, the narrow side of the rectangle faces the front of the lot. In some cases the house is more cubical than rectilinear. The first examples of the Rectilinear, I have called Rectilinear Queen Anne and Rectilinear Romanesque because they carry on the characteristic motifs of that style but express them within a more controlled framework. This is really a stylistic contradiction with the Queen Anne, because the characteristic feature of that type originally was its irregularity in outline. Nevertheless, the Rectilinear Queen Anne does exist in great numbers on Summit Avenue, and there is no denying its presence.

This kind of rectilinear residence crops up in other guises too. The Rectilinear Georgian house is popular, as is the Rectilinear Medieval. To use a simple analogy, we might describe the basic rectilinear house as an unfrosted cake (two layers or three) — the icing is the second part of the stylistic category. If the owner expresses a preference for Georgian, the house is finished with classical columns on the front porch, dentation at the eave line, and a palladian window on the stair landing. If his taste runs to medieval, he may have a Gothic arch in the verge boards of the dormers, capitals on the porch columns copied from Canterbury or Salisbury, with colored and leaded glass in the windows on either side of the fireplace. Occasionally the house is built without decoration, which forced me to invent the category Rectilinear Simplified for the uniced cake.

The most famous house style of the early twentieth century, the Prairie style, is essentially a variant of the Rectilinear. Hasbruck and Sprague refer to it as Early Modern Rectilinear. No examples influenced by the Prairie style appeared on Summit until 1909, when Clarence Johnston designed a simple, stucco Rectilinear at 1376. In 1912, Ellerbe and Round built a house in homage to Wright at 590 Summit. By the 1920s the

The Georgian Revival residence at 2265 Summit (Living Historical Museum).

The Rectilinear-Medieval Dittenhofer house at 705 Summit (Minnesota Historical Society).

only type of Rectilinear house being constructed was the Early Modern type.

The Beebe House at 2022 Summit

The finest Early Modern Rectilinear house on Summit is the Ward Beebe house, designed by George Grant Elmslie in 1912. Elmslie, long a draftsman for Louis Sullivan, finally left the ailing master and his ruined practice to join the firm of Purcell and Feick in Minneapolis in 1910. William Gray Purcell had also worked for a short period for Louis Sullivan but was better known as a popularizer and defender of the new architecture than as a designer in his own right. Feick played only an insignificant role and left the partnership in 1913.

For a few years this firm turned out commissions of

Purcell, Feick and Elmslie designed this house for the Ward Beebe family in 1912 (Minnesota Historical Society).

unusual distinction, including the Merchant's National Bank of Winona, Minnesota, and a pair of related houses, the 1912 Crane house in Woods Hole, Massachusetts, and the Decker house in Minnetonka, Minnesota. The Beebe house was one of several smaller dwellings designed in that same year.

The Beebe house is unpretentious and so blends into the streetscape that few passersby are even aware of its existence, much less its importance. The house seems completely free of applied ornamentation, but is marked by characteristic features of the Prairie style such as the extended, overhanging eaves and casement windows arranged in banks and grouped at the corners.

The Tudor Villa Style

In contrast to the Rectilinear style, one finds an interesting revival of the picturesque occurring after 1905 in a type of house which I have (boldly and recklessly) decided to proclaim as a newly identified species. Since the picturesque tradition was dominated in the nineteenth century by a variety of villa styles, I have called this twentieth-century evocation of the picturesque the Tudor villa.

In our examination of other turn-of-the-century styles, we have already had several occasions to note the popularity of Tudor- and Georgian-inspired designs. They were the source of many Beaux Arts, Rectilinear, and of course, all Georgian Revival dwellings. For whatever reason, things Tudor and Georgian seem to have held a powerful attraction for the Summit Avenue household in the early twentieth century. The Tudor villa is not, like the Beaux Arts house, an imaginative replication of the real thing. Rather, it is an entirely new style characterized by certain Tudor-associated design elements such as half timbering. In contrast to the effect created by Rectilinear houses, the Tudor villa seems to strive for picturesque outline, for an obvious irregularity and violation of symmetry.

The Dittenhofer House at 807 Summit

The Dittenhofer house is an early and especially beautiful Tudor villa designed by Clarence Johnston in 1906.

Clarence Johnston designed this Tudor villa for the Samuel Dittenhofer family at 807 Summit (Minnesota Historical Society).

Basically, the first floor is brick, and the second and third stucco half-timbered, but Johnston has brought the brick work up to third floor on the east half of the front facade, thus unbalancing one element of the design. The entrance is centered on the facade with a third-floor dormer directly above it, but the gables on either end are treated quite differently. The smaller west gable joins the main roof below the ridge level, and the east gable joins the ridge line, its eastern slope becoming the main roof line and being carried down to the level of the first floor. This one-legged gable is found in one third of the Tudor villas on Summit Avenue. The two-story bay window under this gable is another commonly repeated feature of the style and further unbalances the facade. Johnston has also added some fine Beaux Arts touches to the design with stone mullions and window frames on the first floor and an elegant portico and doorway.

Some of the houses categorized as Tudor villas do not fit this basic design form and are, for instance, constructed entirely of brick. But I feel that the repetition of a Tudor-inspired design with strong picturesque tendencies occurs often enough on Summit to deserve some special notice. During the 1920s, the Tudor villa seems to have been perpetuated in another guise which I have called Twenties villa. The shape remains the same, the one-legged gable is often utilized, but the Tudor associations are dropped in favor of Early Modern design motifs. Thus, the Tudor villa seems to pass through the same evolution as the Rectilinear and Georgian Revival styles.

Conclusion

If readers have the opportunity and inclination, they can continue this study of architectural styles with the assistance of the index of styles included in the appendix. Historians have a great deal yet to learn about the variety and distribution of twentieth century house styles. Some of the categorizations made in the index and in this chapter are conjectural and experimental. But if the terms and descriptions are helpful to the student, they will have served their purpose.

Lace insert in a window shade in the Auerbach house, 400 Summit (Brian Wicklund, Living Historical Museum).

CHAPTER 6

F. Scott Fitzgerald's Summit Avenue

F. SCOTT FITZGERALD lived on Summit Avenue. A plaque attests the fact at 599 Summit, the row house in which he lived during the summer of 1919 while revising the manuscript of *This Side of Paradise*. When his publisher accepted the novel, acquaintances have described how Fitzgerald in his ecstasy literally danced down Summit Avenue, stopping friends and strangers to tell them his good news. But Summit Avenue was more to Fitzgerald than merely the setting for his first great success. More and less. In order to understand his own bittersweet relationship to Summit, it is important to understand a little of his family history.

Fitzgerald was born at 481 Laurel Avenue on September 24, 1896, on the first floor of a six-flat building that was comfortable but by no means pretentious. His father was from Baltimore, which probably explains why he named his son Francis Scott Key Fitzgerald — the author of "The Star-Spangled Banner" was a native of Baltimore. Fitzgerald's mother had grown up in St. Paul, the daughter of an Irish immigrant who had become wealthy in the wholesale grocery trade but who had died suddenly before his family could build any social

position out of his success. The widow McQuillan and her daughters remained devoutly Catholic, well provided for, but only tangentially related to the families on Summit Avenue.

Soon after Scott's birth, the Fitzgeralds moved to Buffalo, New York, where they lived until Mr. Fitzgerald lost his job as a salesman. They returned to St. Paul in the summer of 1908 and moved in with Grandmother McQuillan, who then lived at 294 Laurel Avenue close to the Cathedral. Mr. Fitzgerald was never employed again, and the family subsisted on the McQuillan fortune. Scott lived in St. Paul from 1908 when he was just turning twelve until he was sent off to a Catholic prep school in New Jersey for his last two years of high school when he was about sixteen. He attended St. Paul Academy for his first two years of high school and published his first story in the school newspaper. At that time St. Paul Academy was located at Dale Street and Portland Avenue in a building which has since been taken over by the Wilder Foundation.

During these years the Fitzgeralds lived in at least three different houses — the duplex at 514 Holly in 1910, the row house at 509 Holly in 1911, and the

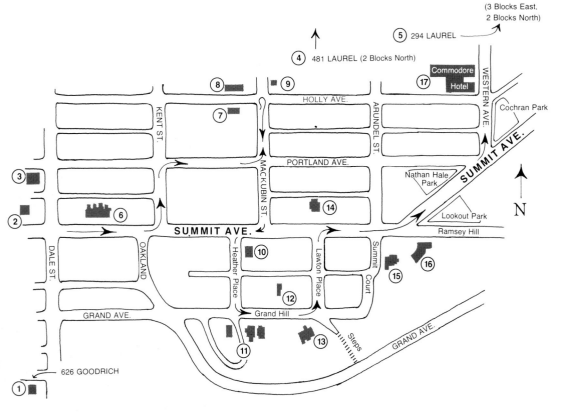

F. Scott Fitzgerald's St. Paul

Scott and Zelda Fitzgerald at White Bear Lake in 1921 (Minnesota Historical Society).

1. **626 Goodrich.** During 1921–22 Scott and Zelda lived here; their daugher spent her first few months here; and most of *The Beautiful and the Damned* was written here.

2. **629 Summit.** Grandmother McQuillan owned this property at the turn of the century, but did not build the house or live here.

3. **St. Paul Academy** (now Wilder Foundation). Scott attended school here for two years about 1911–12, writing some of his first stories for the school paper.

4. **481 Laurel.** FSF birthplace, 24 September 1896. Family left for Buffalo 1898.

5. **294 Laurel.** Grandmother McQuillan's home when the Fitzgerald's moved back to St. Paul in the summer of 1908. This attractive complex was built about 1884 by architects Willcox and Johnston.

6. **593 and 599 Summit.** The Fitzgerald family lived in these two townhouses during and after World War I. Scott lived in 599 during the summer of 1919 when he was writing *This Side of Paradise*. His was the front room on the third floor. He described the place as "a house below the average / on a street above the average."

7. **514 Holly** (white duplex). Fitzgerald family lived here in 1910.

8. **509 Holly.** Fitzgerald family moved here in 1911. These townhouses have recently been completely remodeled.

9. **499 Holly** (now demolished). Fitzgerald family moved here in 1912.

10. **516 Summit.** Sinclair Lewis was living here in 1917–18, while attempting to write a novel about J. J. Hill which he never completed.

11. **506, 514, 520 Grand Hill.** A group of turn-of-the-century houses designed by Cass Gilbert.

12. **501 Grand Hill.** The Ames garden was fondly remembered by FSF as a wonderful place to play.

13. **480 Grand Hill.** In the 1920s, the home of the Frederick Weyerhaeusers.

14. **475 Summit.** In FSF's youth, the home of Mrs. E. L. Hersey, probably the mother of Marie Hersey, the girl who is portrayed as Imogene Bissel in the Basil stories. It was Marie who invited the beautiful Lake Forest deb Genevra King to be her house guest. FSF fell in love with her and eventually turned her into Isabelle in *This Side of Paradise*.

15. **Burbank-Livingston-Griggs House.** Lavishly redone during the 1920s. Now a museum open to the public.

16. **University Club.** Built in 1912, this was the site of dances attended by Scott and Zelda and figures in stories such as "Winter Dreams."

17. **Commodore Hotel.** Attractive Art Deco bar. FSF and Zelda also lived here in 1921.

now-demolished residence at 499 Holly in 1912. While Scott was at Princeton and in the army, the family lived in row houses at 593 and 599 Summit. All of these are modest dwellings, just on the edge of elegance — close enough to the big houses so that Scott would be acquainted with the children who lived there, but always far enough away (physically and socially) for a sensitive boy to feel the difference.

Fitzgerald was evidently fascinated and sometimes repelled by wealth and social position. His stories reflect a preoccupation with the lives of the rich and are often written from the point of view of one (like Nick Carraway in *The Great Gatsby*) who mixes with the rich but does not or cannot completely identify himself with them. This is an accurate reflection of his role in St. Paul during early adolescence.

In 1928–1929, looking back on his adolescence in St. Paul twenty years before, Fitzgerald constructed a series of stories about himself for the *Saturday Evening Post* in which his alter ego was called Basil Duke Lee. Basil attended parties where kissing games were played, masqueraded as a thug to surprise his arch-rival, got his first pair of long pants just in time to go to the state fair, and wrote a play in which his friends acted. In these stories Fitzgerald only occasionally reflected on the geography of St. Paul, as when he described the yard at 501 Grand Hill:

> There were deep shadows there all day long and ever
> something vague in bloom, and patient dogs around,
> and brown spots worn bare by countless circling wheels
> and dragging feet.

In his notebook, however, Fitzgerald did record a description of Summit Avenue which shows how clearly he perceived the whole extent of the street:

> As they turned into Crest Avenue, the new cathedral,
> immense and unfinished in imitation of a cathedral left
> unfinished by accident in some little Flemish town,
> squatted just across the way like a plump white
> bulldog on its haunches. The ghost of four moonlit
> apostles looked down at them wanly from wall niches
> still littered with the white dusty trash of the builders.
> The cathedral inaugurated Crest Avenue. After it came
> the great brownstone mass built by R. R. Comerford,

Fitzgerald lived at 599 Summit during the summer of 1919 while revising This Side Paradise. *(E. D. Becker. Minnesota Historical Society).*

the flour king, followed by a half mile of pretentious stone houses built in the gloomy 90's. These were adorned with monstrous driveways and porte-cocheres which had once echoed to the hoofs of good horses and with high circular windows that corseted the second stories.

The continuity of these mausoleums was broken by a small park, a triangle of grass where Nathan Hale stood ten feet tall, with his hands bound behind his back by stone cord, and stared over a great bluff at the slow Mississippi. Crest Avenue ran along the bluff, but neither faced it nor seemed aware of it, for all the houses fronted inward toward the street. Beyond the first half mile it became newer, essayed ventures in terraced lawns, in concoctions of stucco or in granite mansions which imitated through a variety of gradual refinements the marble contours of the Petit Trianon. The houses of this phase rushed by the roadster for a succession of minutes; then the way turned and the car was headed directly into the moonlight, which swept toward it like the lamp of some gigantic motorcycle far up the avenue.

Fitzgerald's birthplace at 481 Laurel (Minnesota Historical Society).

Past the low Corinthian lines of the Christian Science Temple, past a block of dark frame horrors, a deserted row of grim red brick — an unfortunate experiment of the late 90's — then new houses again, bright blinding flowery lawns. These swept by, faded past, enjoying their moment of grandeur; then waiting there in the moonlight to be outmoded as had the frame, cupolaed mansions of lower town and the brownstone piles of older Crest Avenue in their turn.

The roofs lowered suddenly, the lots narrowed, the houses shrank up in size and shaded off into bungalows. These held the street for the last mile, to the bend in the river which terminated the prideful avenue at the statue of Chelsea Arbuthnot. Arbuthnot was the first governor — and almost the last of Anglo-Saxon blood.

All the way thus far Yanci had not spoken, absorbed still in the annoyance of the evening, yet soothed somehow by the fresh air of Northern November that rushed by them. She must take her fur coat out of storage next day, she thought.

"Where are we now?"

As they slowed down, Scott looked up curiously at the pompous stone figure, clear in the crisp moonlight, with one hand on a book and the forefinger of the other pointing, as though with reproachful symbolism, directly at some construction work going on in the street.

"This is the end of Crest Avenue," said Yanci, turning to him. "This is our show street."

"A museum of American architectural failures."

Aside from the three substitutions of Crest for Summit Avenue, R. R. Comerford for James J. Hill, and the statue of the fictitious Charles Arbuthnot for the war memorial at the end of the avenue, Fitzgerald has faithfully described the avenue on which he lived.

Fitzgerald left St. Paul in 1919 on the first crest of his popularity as a novelist. He returned for about a year during 1921–1922 when Zelda was pregnant with their daughter. Scottie was born while they lived in St. Paul, but when they left in October 1922, they left for good.

Anyone who would like to visit the principal surviving sites of Fitzgerald's youth may follow the map on a pleasant hour-long driving or walking tour. None of the sites except the Commodore Hotel and the University Club is open to the public.

94

Appendix

*A column capital at 294 Laurel,
once a Fitzgerald family residence
(Living Historical Museum).*

Notes and Acknowledgements

Notes

Page

1   J. Wesley Bond, *Minnesota and Its Resources* (New York: Redfield, 1853), p. 109 and 115.

2   Andrew Jackson Downing, *The Architecture of Country Houses* (New York: D. Appleton and Co., 1850).

3   Rebecca Marshall Cathcart, "A Sheaf of Remembrances," *Minnesota Historical Society Collections* 15 (1915): 537–38.

6–7 *Freemasons of St. Paul: A History of Summit Lodge #163, 1884–1917* (St. Paul: privately published, 1918), p. 72, 73, 76.

10   *Porter's Illustrated History of St. Paul* (St. Paul, privately published, 1887), p. 24.

12   William Dean Howells, *The Rise of Silas Lapham* (Boston: Houghton Mifflin Co., 1884), p. 45–47.

76   Information on the lives of St. Paul architects comes, in part, from the University of Minnesota's Northwest Architectural Archive, Alan Lathrop, curator. Information about Clarence Johnston and Cass Gilbert is drawn from Gilbert's correspondence in the Clarence H. Johnston papers, Minnesota Historical Society.

81   Henry-Russell Hitchcock, *The Architecture of H. H. Richardson and His Times* (revised ed., Cambridge: The M.I.T. Press, 1966).

86   Wilbert R. Hasbrouck and Paul E. Sprague, *A Survey of Historic Architecture of the Village of Oak Park, Illinois* (Oak Park, Illinois: Landmarks Commission of the Village of Oak Park, 1974).

93   F. Scott Fitzgerald, *The Basil and Josephine Stories*, edited by Jackson R. Bryer and John Kuehl (New York: Charles Scribner's Sons, 1973).

93   F. Scott Fitzgerald, *The Crack-up*, edited by Edmund Wilson (New York: New Directions Publishing Co., 1945), p. 226–28, quoted with the publisher's permission.

Acknowledgements

David Lanegran and I created the Living Historical Museum in 1974. We felt that the residents of St. Paul and the students in our classes at Macalester College did not possess any very clear sense of the historical environment surrounding them. To build a building and fill it with exhibits seemed not only beyond our means but also unlikely to fulfill our goal. We conceived of the Living Historical Museum as a process, a process of education and enlightenment, a process through which a sense of one's place in history could be generated out of a cooperative effort to find out about the past. Lanegran developed a prospectus for a seminar in comparative neighborhood history, and I a seminar on the history of Summit Avenue. With the aid of a grant from the National Endowment for the Humanities, we offered classes not only to Macalester undergraduates but also to any interested resident of the city. Over one hundred students from the college and community enrolled in one of the two classes devoted to architectural history.

The research on Summit Avenue was tackled by a small army. Descending upon City Hall, one group compiled lists of building permit numbers, retrieved the permits from the vaults, xeroxed them, and refiled them. We set up a file containing a folder for every building on the avenue. Since the city only began issuing permits in

1882, another team worked in the newspaper files of the earlier period, searching for references to house construction, and compiled information out of city directories. We photographed the pertinent pages from the city plat books which indicated location of buildings and, in some cases, names of owners. Comparison of these valuable atlases gave us a good sense of the growth of the avenue. Another team of students took tape recorders into the field and obtained oral histories from some of the oldest inhabitants of the avenue. Records of the fire department, park department, and the county assessor were ransacked for information. Photographers searched the files of the photographic archive of the Minnesota Historical Society for historic photographs and also took photos of every building standing on the avenue.

The research seminar on Summit Avenue was not the best organized class I have taught, but it was certainly the most exciting. This book does not present more than a small fraction of the information which we turned up. The class did not last long enough, unfortunately, for all of the data to be synthesized. In the three years since that course ended, I have continued to work on the history of the avenue, aided actively by some of the community "alumnae" of the course who had been taken with such an addiction for historical research that they could not break the habit. Margaret Redpath and Carol Sawyer were the most persistent and dedicated. They spent weeks at the Historical Society library checking data, pored over the files, and compiled a master list of residents on the avenue. Eventually they wrote the rough draft for the walking tour, chapter 4. It is entirely appropriate that their names appear on the title page of this book.

I should like specifically to thank a number of other people who have contributed to the success of this venture. The staff of the Minnesota Historical Society reference library, manuscript division, and audio-visual library have gone out of their way to accommodate me and my staff; special thanks to Bonnie Wilson. A number of the residents of Summit Avenue and participants in the research seminar did noteworthy work, some of them contributing family photographs to our archive; thank you Loretta Bush, Ariel Davidson, Lillian Finley, Lucy Fricke, and Marie Weist. The staff of the Living Historical Museum was marvelous; Nancy Tracy served as an extraordinarily effective research assistant, Stafford Crossland as an indispensable coordinator; thanks as well to photographers Bill Gilliland, Steve Plattner, and Brian Wicklund; thanks, too, to Carolyn Davis, Steve Niedorf, and Jane Wilson.

In the production of the book, Anne Harbour served as copy editor and Robert Taylor as designer; they have made publication pleasant and interesting. I have saved my final thanks for David Lanegran and Eunice Sandeen. David, a superb teacher and an insightful scholar, possesses an even more precious gift — a zest for life which he shares with his friends unselfishly. My wife has not only sent me off to my study without scolding, but has shared my enthusiasm with a perfect affection that makes my life whole.

List of Houses on Summit Avenue by Address

Address	Year Built	Year Razed or Moved	Estimated Cost	Original Owner	Style	Architect or Contractor (c)
201 (1)	1882	1905	100,000	N. W. Kittson	Second Empire	A. M. Radcliffe
Cathedral	1906-41		1,500,000	Archdiocese	Beaux Arts — Italian Renaissance	E. L. Masqueray
217	c.1874	c.1920		A. H. Terry		
226 (1)	1863	1886		George L. Otis		
226 (2)	1887	1959	77,000	Amherst H. Wilder	Romanesque	Willcox-Johnston
226 (3)	1963			Catholic archdiocese	Contemporary	Cerny Associates
229	1870	1913	6,000	Thomas Cochran, Jr.		
235	1878			Charles P. Noyes	Vernacular-Second Empire	
236 (1)	1867	1882		Thomas M. Newson	Second Empire	
236 (2)	1882	1920s(?)		Francis B. Clarke	Queen Anne	
236 (3)	1963			Catholic archdiocese	Contemporary	Cerny Associates
239	1882			William B. Bend	Remodeled	George Wirth
242 (1)	1855	1887		Edward D. Neill	Italian Villa	
252 (1)	1869	1887		Geo. W. Armstrong		
240 (2)	1887		280,000	James J. Hill	Romanesque	Peabody-Stearns
243	1883	1936	11,000	Henry M. Hart	Second Empire	A. F. Gauger
245	1882		10,000	Charles Paul Henry Morris	Remodeled	A. M. Radcliffe
251 (1)	1866	1886				
251 (2)	1886		24,500	Henry P. Rugg	Romanesque	Hodgson-Stem
255-57	1884			Lane K. Stone and G. B. Bacon	Queen Anne	
260 (1)	1857			William Noble		
260 (2)	1902		40,000	Louis W. Hill	B. A. Georgian	C. H. Johnston
261	1891		14,000	M. M. Kinney	B. A. Gothic	C. H. Johnston
265	1885		10,000	J. S. Robertson	Queen Anne	Mould
266 (1)	1857	1884		Henry Masterson		
266 (2)	1884		25,000	Fred. Driscoll	Queen Anne	Wm. Willcox
271	1882			Joshua Sanders	Tuscan Villa	
275 (1)	1880	1895	9,000	Ansel Oppenheim		
275 (2)	1901		18,000	Chas. Schuneman	Medieval Rect.	C. H. Johnston
276	1884	1930	25,000	Rufus C. Jefferson	Queen Anne	George Wirth
285 (1)	1882	1899	6,500	Henry M. Rice	Second Empire	A. M. Radcliffe
285 (2)	1899		8,500	F. A. Fogg	Georgian Rect.	A. H. Stem
288 (1)	1855	1884		Henry M. Rice		
288 (2)	1884	1930	40,000	A. B. Stickney	Romanesque	J. W. Stevens
294 (1)	1858	1918		Henry N. Paul	Italian Villa	
294 (2)	1919		30,000	Geo. F. Lindsay	Georgian Revival	Parker, Thomas, and Rice
295	1885		13,000	A. H. Lindeke	Queen Anne	A. F. Gauger
301 (1)	1882	1903 (M) (moved to 107 Farrington)	7,500	Alex. J. Stone	Vernacular-Second Empire	A. F. Gauger
301 (2)	1905		28,000	George Gardner	B. A. Georgian	Thos. Holyoke
302	1889		24,000	Jos. Forepaugh	Queen Anne	Mould-McNicol
312	1858			David Stuart	Italian Villa	
315	1882	1937	12,000	W. P. Warner		James K. Taylor
318	1893		27,000	Wm. H. Lightner	Romanesque	Cass Gilbert
323 (1)	1863	1892		John W. Roche		
323 (2)	1892		35,000	Edw. N. Saunders	Romanesque	C. H. Johnston
322-24	1886		23,000	Geo. B. Young and Wm. H. Lightner	Romanesque	Gilbert and Taylor
329	1895		15,000	C. A. Wheaton	Queen Anne Rect.	
332	1889		30,000	Edgar Long	Romanesque	Gilbert and Taylor
335	1892		25,000	J. H. Allen	Queen Anne Rect.	J. W. Stevens
339	1898		14,000	Crawford Livingston	Medieval Rect.	Cass Gilbert
340	1894		40,000	Thomas B. Scott	B. A. Renaissance	A. H. Stem
344 (1)	1886	1914	8,000	Sam. M. Magoffin	Queen Anne	George Wirth
344 (2)	1915		40,000	W. P. Davidson	B. A. Tudor	Thos. Holyoke
345 (1)	1882	1904 (M)	15,000	A. K. Barnum	Tuscan Villa	
345 (2)	1909		25,000	A. W. Lindeke	Tudor Villa	C. H. Johnston
353	1882		15,000	Wm. B. Dean	Queen Anne remodeled	
354	1886	1914 (?)	12,000	Mary W. Otis	Queen Anne	Willcox-Johnston

List of Houses on Summit Avenue by Address

Address	Year Built	Year Razed or Moved	Estimated Cost	Original Owner	Style	Architect or Contractor (c)
360 (1)	1875	1968	6,000	Edw. H. Cutler	Tuscan Villa	
360 (2)	1969			Walter Fricke	Carriage house	Jos. Michels
362-4 (3)	1977			Design Consult-ants	Contempo-rary	Design Con-sultants
361 (1)	1882	1912 (M)	6,000	C. S. Bunker		Geo. Wirth
361 (2)	1912		12,000	Donald S. Culver	Tudor Villa	Peter J. Linhoff
365	1891		20,000	Mrs. J. W. Bass	Queen Anne Rect.	James K. Taylor
366 (1)	1884	1924	20,000	Daniel R. Noyes	Queen Anne	H. R. Marshall
366 (2)	1928		125,000	Egil Boeckman	B. A. Geor-gian	David Adler-Robert Work
370	1909			John R. Mitchell	B. A. Geor-gian	C. H. Johnston
378	1863	1957		Charles Emerson	Italian Villa	
400	1882			M. Auerbach	Queen Anne	George Wirth
401	c.1885	1890s		Porter (?) now Nathan Hale Park		
403	c.1885	1905		Carpenter (?) now Nathan Hale Park		
410	1858	1880s		Carpenter's Hotel		
415	1882		8,500	William R. Marshall		
420	1912		100,000	University Club		Reed and Stem
421 (1)	1882	1912		Joseph Wheelock		
421 (2)	1912		22,500	E. J. Buxton	B. A. Ren-aissance	Marshall-Fox
432	1862			James C. Burbank	Italian Villa	Otis E. Wheelock
435 (1)	1877	1896		W. A. Culbertson	Tuscan Villa	
435 (2)	1896	1938	28,000	Michael Doran	Queen Anne Rect.	Thomas Fitz-patrick
435 (3)	1954		28,000	Chester Berry	Contempo-rary	Chas. J. Beggs (c)
442 (1)	1876	1890s		William Carson		
442 (2)	1898				Apartment	
445	1882			Shipman/Greve	Queen Anne	
456	1966		130,000		Contemporary	Paul Mueller
465	1886		18,400	William Constans	Queen Anne	A. F. Gauger
470	1919		30,000	C. J. McCon-ville	Spanish Colonial	Mark Fitz-patrick
475	1883			James Gamble	Queen Anne	George Wirth
476	1883		35,000	C. W. Griggs	Romanesque	C. H. Johnston
485	1907		12,500	Jas. A. McLeod	Tudor Villa	J. A. McLeod
490	1883		23,000	A. G. Foster	Romanesque	C. H. Johnston
495	1881			C. B. Thurston	Queen Anne	
500	1904		8,000	Dr. C. Williams	Georgian Revival	Thos. Holyoke
505	1896		20,000	G. W. Freeman	Medieval Rect.	Cass Gilbert
506	c.1911	(moved here from 361 Summit)			Georgian Rect.	
513	1891		10,000	W. W. Bishop	Queen Anne	John McDon-ald (c)
516 (1)	c.1885	1914		Edw. Simonton		
516 (2)	1914		8,000?	William Butler	B. A. Ren-aissance	Butler Bros (c)
520	1882	1912	6,500	W. H. H. Johnston		A. M. Rad-cliffe
525	1885	1970	8,000	James King	Tuscan Villa	A. F. Gauger
533	1902		20,000	B. H. Evans	B. A. Ren-aissance	John Rohde (c)
534	1882		9,000	W. J. S. Trail		A. M. Rad-cliffe
540	1879	1938		W. D. Cornish		
541	1888	1970s	10,000	W. S. Dal-rymple		Mould-Mc-Nichol
545 (1)	1886	1944	20,000	Andrew Muir	Tuscan Villa	A. F. Gauger
545 (2)	?	(moved here in 1954 from 554 Holly)				
550	1898		30,000	Alan Black	Apartment	Alan Black
555	1884	1970	10,000	Will Rhodes	Queen Anne(?)	C. H. Johnston
573	1926		10,000	W. D. Blum-menthal	Twenties Villa	
574	1904			G. D. Taylor	Medieval Rect.	
579	1895		21,000	Herman Kretz	Apartment	Herman Kretz
587-601	1889		48,000	Farrar and Howe	Romanesque	Willcox-John-ston
590	1913		10,000	G. Oppenheim	Prairie Rect.	Ellerbe-Round
596-604	1890		45,000	Farrar-Howes	Romanesque	C. H. Johnston
610	1927		70,000	Cities Hous-ing Corp.	Apartment	Ganley Bros. (c)
611	1909		15,000	C. C. DeCoster	Tudor Rect.	J. M. Carlson (c)
615		(moved here in 1948)			Twenties Villa	
616	1927		70,000	Cities Hous-ing Corp.	Apartment	Ganley Bros. (c)
623	1896			Louisa McQuillan		
624 (1)	1874	1896				
624 (2)	1899			Charles H. Schliek	Queen Anne	
629 (1)	c.1874	1893				
629 (2)	1896		7,000	Nellie Kirke	Medieval Rect.	C. H. Johnston

List of Houses on Summit Avenue by Address

Address	Year Built	Year Razed or Moved	Estimated Cost	Original Owner	Style	Architect or Contractor (c)
635	1926		13,000	Robert C. Wright(?)		
638	1894			A. H. Schliek	Queen Anne Rect.	
644	1889		12,000	Charles A. Dibble	Queen Anne Rect.	Havelock E. Hand
649	1874			A. G. Manson	Second Empire	
650	1892		8,000	Gen. C. C. Andrews	Georgian Rect.	C. H. Johnston
656	1892		8,000	Gen. C. C. Andrews	Georgian Rect.	C. H. Johnston
659	1885		8,000	Lillie June Bartlett	Queen Anne	D. B. Spear
660	1925		8,500	Raoul Reed	Early Mod. Rect.	Raoul Reed (c)
665	1889		6,000	C. E. Ritterhouse	Queen Anne	E. J. Hodgson
666	1925		8,500	Raoul Reed	Early Mod. Rect.	Raoul Reed (c)
669	1889		7,000	Dr. J. C. Schadle	Queen Anne	Mould & McNicol
672-76	1900		54,300	Hermann Kretz	Apartment	Hermann Kretz
677			(moved here in 1959 from 637 N. Lexington)		Georgian Revival	
683	1895		16,000	Dr. J. C Schadle	Georgian Revival	
684	1893		25,000	Joseph Lockey	Romanesque	Hermann Kretz
692	1912		5,700	Misses Gliney	Simp. Rect.	B. J. Taylor
			(moved here in 1936 from 736 Holly)			
696	1963		13,500	Empire Realty	Bungalow	Alladin Improve. (c)
700-702	1919		8,000	D. E. Foley		Walter Stevens
701	1898		13,500	A. H. Elsinger	Medieval Rect.	C. H. Johnston
705	1898		14,648	Jacob Dittenhofer	Medieval Rect.	Cass Gilbert
704-706	1919		8,000	D. E. Foley		Walter Stevens
710-712	1888		12,000	C. Stocking	Queen Anne (?)	
720-722			(moved here in 1957 from 908 Portland)			
726	1903		7,500	C. F. Arral	Simplified Rect.	Louis Lockwood
732				Church of Christ	Contemporary	
739	1913		70,000	First Church of Christ, Scientist	Neo-Classical	C. H. Johnston
749	1888		22,000	Rush B. Wheeler	Queen Anne	Willcox & Johnston
755	1902	1974	12,500	H. E. Hulehinge		Louis Lockwood
760	1892	1938	22,000	P. F. Bowlin	Romanesque	C. H. Johnston
761	1904		20,000	G. Bohn	Eclectic Rect.	Lauer Bros. (c)
768	1900		11,000	Mrs. H. Kretz	Queen Anne Rect.	Herman Kretz
776	1901		6,000	M. J. McCarty	Queen Anne Rect.	J. W. Stevens
779	1893	1956	17,000	W. F. Graves		C. H. Johnston
780	1909		8,500	Clarence A. Waldon	Queen Anne Rect.	Sundburg
786	1905		14,000	J. T. Landers	Queen Anne Rect.	Louis Lockwood
790	c.1910			J. C. Hammond	Simplified Rect.	
796	c.1910			Frank Dodson (?)	Simplified Rect.	
797	1913		250,000	House of Hope Presbyterian Church	B. A. Tudor	Cram, Goodhue, Ferguson
807	1906		30,000	S. W. Dittenhofer	Tudor Villa	C. H. Johnston
808	1903		35,000	H. E. Thompson	B. A. Renaissance	Green-Wicks
818	1916		10,000	F. W. Hurty	Tudor Villa	Olson-Erickson (c)
821 (1)	pre1885	1910				
821 (2)	1910		50,000	Charles L. Johnston	B. A. Tudor	J. W. Stevens
828	1956		15,000	J. A. Ingemann	Contemporary	Wm. Ingemann
833	?	1956 (M)				
834	1912		37,000	E. N. Saunders, Jr.	Geo. Revival (variant)	F. C. Norlander (c)
842	1898		5,000	Charles Straus	Queen Anne Rect.	Louis Lockwood
	1953			Summit Avenue Assembly of God	Contemporary	
846	1898		6,000	Jacob Wertheimer	Queen Anne Rect.	Herman Kretz
850	c.1960				Contemporary	Gretsfeld Const. (?)
854-56	1960	1975 (M)	20,000	Robert Fraser	Contemporary	Gretsfeld Const. (c)
857	pre1885	razed?		Joerg		
862-864	1922		6,500	Am. Building Co.	Georgian Revival	Am. Building Co. (c)
866-868	1922		6,500	Am. Building Co.	Georgian Revival	Am. Building Co. (c)
875			Presently William Mitchell College of Law			

List of Houses on Summit Avenue by Address

Address	Year Built	Year Razed or Moved	Estimated Cost	Original Owner	Style	Architect or Contractor (c)
880	1923		15,000	F. C. Norlander (moved here in 1950 from 894 Summit)	Bungalow	F. C. Norlander
922				St. Paul's United Church of Christ	Bungalow	
926	1928		9,000	Dr. J. C. Whitacre	Bungalow	C. Hamm (c)
929	1890		16,000	Dr. A. Wharton	Queen Anne	A. H. Stem
934	1906		8,500	C. P. Waldon	Queen Anne Rect.	C. P. Waldon (c)
937	1899		7,000	J. A. Humbird	Queen Anne Rect.	Cass Gilbert
942	1908		25,000	C. P. Waldon	Eclectic Rect.	P. J. Linhoff
943	1899		7,000	J. A. Humbird	Georgian Rect.	Cass Gilbert
952	1914		22,000	Charles Beckhoefer	Tudor Villa	Thos. Holyoke
955	1904		26,000	C. N. Boynton	Jacobean Rect.	C. H. Johnston
965	1901		11,000	Geo. Prince	Georgian Revival	Louis Lockwood
966	1902		8,000	A. Slimmer	Queen Anne Rect.	Louis Lockwood
976	1911		13,250	Howard Johnson	Tudor Villa	C. H. Johnston
977	1924		25,000	L. Silverstein	B. A. Federal Rev.	Peter J. Linhoff
985	1895		16,000	J. A. Wilson	Queen Anne Rect.	J. H. Hickel (c)
986	1904		15,000	L. A. Guiterman	Queen Anne Rect.	C. H. Johnston
990	1916		20,000	Harry G. Allers	Georgian Revival	Thos. Holyoke
1003	1891		15,000	J. H. Burwell	Queen Anne Rect.	A. H. Stem
1006	1910		50,000	H. H. Irvine	B. A. Tudor	Wm. C. Whitney
1009	1901		12,000	Wm. Bannon	Queen Anne Rect.	Louis Lockwood
1017 (1)	pre	1912				
1017 (2)	1913			P. J. Bowlin	Georgian Revival	Hartford-Jacobson
1027	1915		16,000	Hopewell Clarke	Simplified Rect.	Peter J. Linhoff
1034 (1)	pre1885	1905		F. A. Ring		
1034 (2)	1906		25,000	Wm. O'Brien	Medieval Rect.	Louis Lockwood
1035 (1)	1901	1964		Jacob Danz	Queen Anne Rect.	Louis Lockwood
1035 (2)	1965		358,000	St. Luke's Convent	Contemporary	
1042	1020		6,500	McAnulty Co.	Bungalow	McAnulty Co. (c)
1046	1920		8,000	Platt B. Walker	Tudor Villa	McAnulty Co. (c)
1058	1909		5,100	H. S. Dodson (moved here in 1952 from 44 N. Lexington)	Twenties Villa	J. C. Burdin (c)
1064	1950s				Contemporary	
1065				St. Luke's School		
1068	1959		24,000	Estella Arend	Contemporary	Charles Arend (c)
1079 (1)	1911	1951	15,000	E. A. Webb		A. L. Garlough
1079 (2)	1952			Rectory of St. Luke's Church	Contemporary	
1082	c.1910			W. O. Washburn	Tudor Villa	
1088	1922		7,500	Am. Building Co.	Early Mod. Rect.	Am. Building Co.
1093 (1)	1891	1917 (M)	10,000	Mrs. Topping		E. P. Bassford
1092 (2)	1924		400,000	St. Luke's Church	Gothic Revival	Comes, Perry, McMullen
1096	1922		6,500	Am. Building Co.	Dutch Colonial	Am. Building Co.
1106	1911		12,500	Minnie F. Lennon	Tudor Villa	Peter J. Linhoff
1111 (1)	1901	1967	17,000	S. C. Stickney	Georgian Revival	J. W. Stevens
1111 (2)	1967		150,000	St. George's Greek Orthodox Church	Byzantine Revival	Voight-Fourre
1118	1902		5,000	Dr. Knox Bacon	Queen Anne Rect.	Louis Lockwood
1126	1905		15,000	L. C. Jefferson	Tudor Villa	St. Paul Building Co. (c)
1127	1891	1929		Smith & Taylor		John Haulen (c)
1134	c.1912				Early Mod. Rect.	
1135	1905		17,000	T. D. McLaughlin	Eclectic Rect.	Louis Lockwood
1141	1919		12,000		Tudor Villa	C. H. Johnston
1142	1912		8,500	Charles A. Roach		
1149	1904		6,000	O. G. Hasper	Simplified Rect.	Buchner & Orth
1153	1925		10,000	D. J. Hertz	Twenties Villa	Gus Lindgren (?)
1156	1907		12,000	Geo. R. Holmes	Classical Rect.	C. A. Bassford

List of Houses on Summit Avenue by Address

Address	Year Built	Year Razed or Moved	Estimated Cost	Original Owner	Style	Architect or Contractor (c)
1157	1924		14,220	Dr. K. C. Walde	Tudor Villa	Peter J. Linhoff
1164	1914		17,000	A. P. Wallich	Medieval Rect.	Alden & Harris
1165	1927		18,000	F. M. Fogg	Georgian Revival	Lundstrom & Anderson (c)
1171	1925		7,500	Otto N. Raths	Early Mod. Rect.	F. J. Eder (c)
1179	1915		7,500	John McDevett	Simplified Rect.	F. Sjostrand (c)
1180	1909		5,500	Geo. F. van Slyke	Tudor Villa	Peter J. Linhoff
1186	1916		3,800	McAnulty Co.	Dutch Colonial	McAnulty Co.
1189	Early 1880s				Vernacular-Stick (?)	
1190	1909		6,000	Conrad O. Searle		Conrad Searle
1195	c. 1950s				Contemporary	
1200	1921		10,000	M. Rossman	Early Mod. Rect.	L. Fridman (c)
1205	1922		15,000	W. F. Keefe	Early Mod. Rect.	W. F. Keefe
1206	1926		8,000	O. E. Keller	E. M. Geo. Revival	B. J. Raak (c)
1209	1911		3,500	Homer H. Hoyt	Bungalow	Homer H. Hoyt (c)
1211	1922		10,000	Frances W. Gates	Early Mod. Rect.	F. W. Gates (c)
1212	1956		15,000	Warren Arend	Contemporary	Warren Arend
1213	1922		12,000	Margaret Rann	Early Mod. Rect.	Jens Pedersen
1218	1950s				Bungalow	
1220	1909		3,000	John McCardy	Simplified Rect.	A. L. Garlough
1255	1900	1942	14,000	P. P. Cawley		E. J. Donohue
1285	1924		12,000	Edwin Rydeen	Georgian Revival	Edwin Rydeen (c)
1289-91			(moved here in 1960)		Cont. Geo. Revival	
1297			(moved here in 1960)		Cont. Geo. Revival	
1300	1951		500,000	Mt. Zion Temple	Contemporary	Eric Mendelsohn
1317	1895		8,000	Julia B. Dibble	Queen Anne Rect.	C. H. Johnston
1325 (1)	1890	1926	5,000	W. G. Edwards	Queen Anne	W. G. Rice
1325 (2)	1950s				Contemporary	
1335	1920		20,000	Walter Butler	Georgian Revival	Linhoff-Zilger
1344	c. 1900				Queen Anne Rect.	
1347-1345	1900		25,000	Walter & Pierce Butler	B. A. Dutch Renaissance	C. H. Johnston
1352	1899		10,000	Joseph M. Dickson	Queen Anne Rect.	O. Hahn
1353	1954		16,000	Wm. Segal	Contemporary	Bream & Son (c)
1358	1918		5,000	E. Barenson (?)	Simplified Rect.	Johnson-Schwartz (c)
1364	1899		6,000	F. J. Errett	Queen Anne Rect.	Louis Lockwood
1365	1927		7,500	William Filben	Tudor Villa	Wm. Larsen (c)
1366	1910		6,500	F. A. Upham		Gust Anderson (c)
1373	1890		12,000	T. E. Yerxa	Georgian Rect.	Malcom McKay (c)
1374	1889		5,000	Perry Smith	Queen Anne	Adams, Dewey & Smith
1376	1909		5,500	Rush B. Wheeler	Early Mod. Rect.	C. H. Johnston
1381	1899		3,000	Mrs. B. Knuppe	Simplified Rect.	Louis Lockwood
1382	1899		3,625	Clarence H. Slocum	Queen Anne Rect.	Louis Lockwood
1389	1952		12,000	Yale Libman	Contemporary	Norman Johnson
1390	1922		10,000	J. C. Fitzgerald	Georgian Revival	Geo. W. Blood
1393	1923		15,000	J. M. Gaffney	Twenties Villa	Wm. M. Lindau
1396	1924		15,500	F. Hildred	Georgian Revival	Wm. Murphy & Son
1397	1922		15,000	S. J. Melady	Dutch Colonial	Wright & Hausler
1400	1913		8,000	Geo. Bookstover	Tudor Villa	Peter J. Linhoff
1405	c. 1910			G. C. Bohn	Tudor Villa	
1410	1907		9,000	Wm. David Stewart	Tudor Villa	Louis Lockwood
1411	1900		4,300	John A. Swenson	Simplified Rect.	Louis Lockwood
1414	1908		4,500	C. J. Stevens	Tudor Rect.	C. M. Brettschneider (c)
1415	1918		8,000	Chas. B. Gedney	Bungalow	Thomas D. Lane (c)
1420	1925		9,000	Bergland	E. M. Georgian Rev.	
1425	1913		7,000	F. M. Owens	Georgian Revival	P. J. Linhoff

List of Houses on Summit Avenue by Address

Address	Year Built	Year Razed or Moved	Estimated Cost	Original Owner	Style	Architect or Contractor (c)
1428	1919		12,000	F. L. Cronhardt	E. M. Georgian Rev.	P. J. Linhoff
1431	1930s				Twenties Villa	
1434	1910		12,000	H. G. Stock	Tudor Villa	Buchner & Orth
1439	1925		12,000	Ben L. Kostuck	Early Mod. Rect.	Blumenthal (c)
1440	1914		11,000	Mrs. B. H. Dickerman	Tudor Villa	Sjostrand (c)
1445	1925		14,000	Harry L. Brown	Georgian Rect.	Walter Stevens (c)
1446	1906		6,000	Chas. F. Diether	Queen Anne Rect.	Louis Lockwood
1451	1929		10,000	Phil Justus	Tudor Villa	Phil Justus (c)
1456	1912		14,500	A. J. Shapira	Tudor Villa	C. H. Johnston
1459	1922		12,000	R. A. Walsh	Georgian Revival	John Wheeler
1464	1906		12,000	T. D. Lovering	Medieval Rect.	Mark Fitzpatrick
1465	1926		27,000	Mrs. W. W. Klingman	Georgian Revival	
1472	c.1950s				Contemporary	
1473	1904		4,000	F. A. Upham	Queen Anne Rect.	E. Sekall (c)
1480	1929		16,000	Harry L. Brown	Tudor Villa	Jay Axelrod (c)
1481	1905		6,000	J. H. Donahue	Medieval Rect.	E. J. Donahue
1484	1922		15,000	Dr. S. N. Mogilner	Early Mod. Rect.	Wright & Hausler
1487	1910		5,000	F. E. Mahler	Geo. Rev. variant	Morton Fenstad (c)
1489	1960		38,000	Em. Lutheran Church	Contemporary	Philip Agnew
1490	1911		5,900	E. Hunt	Tudor Rect.	Hartford-Jacobson
1493	1909		6,500	Geo. D. Taylor	Tudor Villa	O. H. Round
1494	1885		900	Jos. D. Tyler		R. H. Tyler
1501	1922		12,000	M. M. Seward	Early Mod. Rect.	Palmer
1504	1911			G. E. Routh	E. M. Georgian Rev.	Hartford-Jacobson
1509	1922			M. M. Seward	Early Mod. Rect.	Palmer
1510	1907		7,000	Dr. Chas R. Ball	Queen Anne Rect.	Charles E. Johnson (c)
1515	1906			Arthur W. Wallace	Queen Anne Rect.	Louis Lockwood
1516	1908		7,000	Walter F. Lindeke	Queen Anne Rect.	Peter J. Linhoff
1524	1913		65,000	St. Paul's Episcop. Church	Gothic Revival	E. L. Masqueray
1525	1910		15,000	Dr. Arthur Sweeney	Georgian Revival	Minn. Investment Co. (c)
1537	1925		15,000	L. Lampert, Jr.	Georgian Revival	Gust Anderson (c)
1543	1913		12,500	C. F. Phillips	Tudor Villa	Sjostrand (c)
1550	1950s			Immaculate Heart Church and School		
1559	1920		15,000	Celia Friedman	Early Mod. Rect.	P. J. Linhoff
1567	1906		6,500	J. J. Dobson	Tudor Villa	Mark Fitzpatrick
1568	c.1920				Georgian Revival	
1575	1908		18,000	Harry Drauger	Georgian Rect.	C. M. Brettschneider (c)
1576	1914		15,300	Hugo Hurschman	Tudor Villa	P. J. Linhoff
1583	1925		10,000	M. A. Tschida	E. M. Georgian Rev.	Jos. Tietz (c)
1586	1885	1950s	7,500	Macalester College	Vernacular-Stick	G. W. & F. D. Orff
1591	1904		6,500	Frank J. Waterous	Queen Anne Rect.	Thos. Ivey (c)
1596	1885	1950s	3,500	Macalester College	Vernacular-Stick	G. W. & F. D. Orff
1600				Macalester College		
1605	1905		10,000	S. A. Anderson	Queen Anne Rect.	E. F. Klinkerfuss (c)
1617	1906		7,000	Mrs. May Mather Gilliam	Simplified Rect.	A. Koerner (c)
1620	1885	1890s	3,500	Macalester College	Vernacular-Stick	G. W. & F. D. Orff
1621	1920s				Tudor Rect.	
1623	1914		5,000	D. Simon		B. Schmuckler (c)
1624	1885	c.1910	3,500	Macalester College	Vernacular-Stick	G. W. & F. D. Orff
1635	1907		11,000	W. H. Ivins	Simplified Rect.	C. H. Johnston
1644	1926			Macalester College	Georgian Revival	
1645	1922		18,000	Dr. Robt. Earl	Georgian Revival	J. O. Cederburg
1649	1922		20,000	Fred Anderson	B. A. Renaissance	Lund Wirth
1652	1890		8,500	Macalester Presbyt. Church	Queen Anne	

List of Houses on Summit Avenue by Address

Address	Year Built	Year Razed or Moved	Estimated Cost	Original Owner	Style	Architect or Contractor (c)
1665	1924		17,000	Wm. Harris	Tudor Villa	H. M. Elmer (c)
1671			presently St. Paul Area Council of Churches			
1683	1911		4,500	Orville Helgeson	Tudor Villa	Gust Anderson (c)
1695	c.1925				Georgian Revival	
1700	1887			Ramsey Jr. High School		
1705	1910		14,000	L. A. Weidenborner	Simplified Rect.	H. M. Seby (c)
1713	1908		9,000	F. B. Strunz	Tudor Villa	John R. Schmit (c)
1719	1925		19,000	Wilfred Johnson	Tudor Villa	H. M. Elmer (c)
1722	1886		3,400	P. T. Jackson	Verancular-Stick	Brack & Bros.
1725	1915		7,500	Louis F. Shaw	E. M. Georgian Rev.	Hartford-Hausler
1726	1906		5,000	Mrs. Francis J. Connell	Queen Anne Rect.	Louis Lockwood
1731	1912		4,500	George G. Whitney	Twenties Villa	Allen W. Jackson
1732	1909		5,000	R. H. Gerig	Simplified Rect.	P. J. Linhoff
1737	1913		7,200	S. L. Shapiro	Simplified Rect.	Eugene Schmidt (c)
1740	1909		4,200	Dr. J. C. Nelson	Tudor Villa	Mark Fitzpatrick
1749	1912		6,500	J. G. Robertson (moved here in 1926 from 1668 Summit)	Tudor Villa	
1750	1924		16,000	L. D. Coddon	Twenties Villa	Lindstrom-Anderson (c)
1753	1926		20,000	Reuben Blumberg	Tudor Villa	H. M. Elmer (c)
1760	1922		7,450	Mrs. Mae Weiss Fox	Early Mod. Rect.	J. W. Lindstrom
1761	1916		15,000	R. B. Whitacre	Tudor Rect.	S. M. Bartlett
1770	1915		10,000	Geo. S. McLeod	Early Mod. Rect.	Ralph Mather
1773	1910		7,000	J. L. Sullwold	Tudor Villa	F. J. Jenny (c)
1774	1922		15,000	Sam Friedman	Tudor Villa	C. F. Rule Const. (c)
1779	1925		12,000	Mrs. Thos. M. Furniss	Tudor Villa	Peterson-Lang (c)
1788	1913		8,500	P. Waendler	Simplified Rect.	H. M. Elmer (c)
1789	1917		12,000	Mrs. M. E. Monkhouse	Georgian Rev. variant	C. H. Johnston
1795	1951		22,000	Mary & Francis Donnelly	Contemporary	L. W. Santa
1798	1910		4,500	Ida & Alice Mathews	Simplified Rect.	C. A. Fowble (c)
1799	1957		16,000	M. Donnelly	Contemporary	Antler Corp. (c)
1800	1910		3,450	W. E. Collins	Simplified Rect.	W. E. Collins (c)
1801	1938		10,000	J. B. Forrest	Georgian Revival	A. G. Erickson (c)
1811	1938		11,000	J. B. Forrest	Georgian Revival	A. G. Erickson (c)
1812	1914		5,500	C. E. Bergman	Tudor Rect.	Olai Haugen (c)
1815	1938		9,000	J. B. Forrest	Contemporary	A. G. Erickson (c)
1818	1916		5,000	Bernard P. Rosenstein	Early Mod. Rect.	Wyrell & Steward
1825	1911		5,000	Louisa Lindeke	Simplified Rect.	Martin Fenstad (c)
1826	1912		10,000	H. G. Graaf	Tudor Villa	S. A. Nicholson (c)
1831	1928			Wm. W. Kennedy	Spanish Colonial	Robert C. Martin
1834	1906		3,500	John W. Nabersberg	Simplified Rect.	F. L. Breitkreutz (c)
1837	1949		20,000	Morris H. Wax	Contemporary	
1838	1921		15,000	A. H. Holler	Twenties Villa	C. K. Carpenter
1844	1922		10,000	A. D. Cumming	Early Mod. Rect.	
1845	1969/70		20,000	Ruth Cukier	Contemporary	Sam Cukier (c)
1846	1914		4,600	J. J. Hawkins	Simplified Rect.	Nich. Steinmetz (c)
1850	1907		4,500	Bertha Hinners	Simplified Rect.	F. L. Breitkreutz (c)
1855	1916		15,000	B. M. Hirschman	Classical Rect.	Ralph Mather
1858	1912		5,500	Ben Weed	Georgian Revival	P. J. Linhoff
1865	1922		9,000	Jens Pedersen	Early Mod. Rect.	Jens Pedersen
1866	1912		5,000	E. J. Daly	Bungalow	E. J. Donahue
1873	1912		8,000	Lytton Shields	Early Mod. Rect.	C. H. Johnston
1874	1928		18,000	G. A. Aston	Tudor Villa	F. O. Peterson (c)
1883	1910		10,000	J. R. Fry	Tudor Villa	H. J. Frandson (c)

Address	Year Built	Year Razed or Moved	Estimated Cost	Original Owner	Style	Architect or Contractor (c)
1884	1931		16,500	A. S. Fine	Spanish Colonial	Jacob Fine (c)
1889	1926		18,225	A. L. Goffstein	Twenties Villa	Jay Axelrod (c)
1890	1926		9,000	W. J. Giberson	Georgian Revival	N. G. Persson (c)
1894	1924		12,500	N. Ogden	Tudor Villa	G. A. Anderson (c)
1896	1925		13,500	A. Johnson	Twenties Villa	Nelson Benson (c)
1897	1910		9,000	T. C. Fulton	Tudor Villa	H. J. Frandson (c)
1902	1928		15,000	P. J. McGuire	Twenties Villa	Ben Lindahl (c)
1905	1928		15,000	W. J. Huch	Spanish Colonial	Allen Wall (c)
1906	1926		12,500	A. N. Thome		A. S. Thome (c)
1911	1928		8,000	Jo. Bruffruder	Twenties Villa	Carl R. Peterson (c)
1912	1911		6,000	Warren Seely	Early Mod. Rect.	C. A. Pear
1916	1926		13,000	Dr. Tilendaier	Early Mod. Rect.	O. H. Rundquist (c)
1917	1925		20,000	Feldstein & Miller	Twenties Villa	Feldstein & Miller (c)
1920	1931		12,000	Dr. M. N. Moss	Spanish Colonial	Sal. Goldie (c)
1923	1926		20,000	E. A. Jackson	Tudor Villa	Liebenberg-Kaplan (c)
1926	1925		8,000	Carolyn Dohs	Early Mod. Rect.	C. A. Lee Co. (c)
1935	1922		10,000	F. Olkon	Early Mod. Rect.	W. D. Blumenthal (c)
1936	1912		6,000	V. Ingemann	Tudor Villa	Ingemann Co. (c)
1941	1925		18,000	J. L. Hoffman	Twenties Villa	
1943	1913		10,000	Louis L. Dow	Tudor Villa	C. H. Johnston
1944	1912		9,000	Dr. J. C. Nelson	Tudor Villa	Arthur C. Clausen
1950	1911		3,200	F. J. George	Bungalow	Ellerbe-Round
1953	1919		10,500	L. A. Weidenborner	E. M. Georgian Rev.	Morin Westmark
1954	1950s			Wm. J. Saint Onge (?)	Contemporary	
1959	1924		10,000	Geo. K. Gann	Tudor Villa	Mather & Fleischbein
1960	1950s			Valentine O'Malley(?)	Bungalow	
1964	1955		18,000	Chas. Miller	Cont. Georgian Rev.	Roy A. Spande
1969	1925		16,000	Edw. G. Riedel	Tudor Villa	H. M. Elmer
1978	1913		7,000	Geo. T. Withy	Tudor Villa	P. J. Linhoff
1979	1924		24,000	Moses Shapira	E. M. Georgian Rev.	C. H. Johnston, Jr.
1982	1910		4,000	B. F. Robertson	Early Mod. Rect.	Hartford & Jacobson
1987	1916		12,000	S. R. Reuter	Tudor Villa	Carl Nelson (c)
1988	1914		6,000	J. A. Childs		J. B. Willes
1994	1913		8,000	A. M. P. Cowley	Twenties Villa	J. W. Stevens
1995	1917		8,000	Edw. Kennan	Simplified Rect.	H. Edward Walker
2004	1910		7,500	J. J. Cornevaux	Tudor Villa	J. S. Sweitzer (c)
2005	1924			A. H. Auger (?)	Early Mod. Rect.	
2007	1924		10,000	B. L. Karon	Georgian Revival	
2010	1910		20,000	Frederic Crosby	Tudor Villa	C. H. Johnston
2015	1921		20,600	J. J. Cornevaux	Georgian Revival	Alden & Harris
2020	1913		7,500	C. A. Taney	Early Mod. Rect.	A. L. Garlough
2022	1912		9,000	Ward L. Beebe	(Prairie) E. M. Rect.	Purcell-Feick-Elmslie
2029	1925		30,000		Spanish Colonial	Wm. Harris
2032	1936		10,000	J. P. Kennedy	Tudor Villa	J. A. Deutschlander (c)
2037	1928		15,000	Morris Fineberg	Twenties Villa	Gustave Wiegner (c)
2038	1949		22,000	John D. Asselin	Bungalow	Private plans
2045	1936		11,800	J. J. Levine	B. A. French Chateau	Car-Dell Co. (c)
2048	1919		12,500	Charles Coddon	E. M. Georgian Rev.	Henry Firmenger
2052	1912		4,500	Bernard Druck	Bungalow	Rundquist
2055	c.1926			J. Lisle Jesmer	Georgian Revival	
2056	1924		15,000	Nathan Coddon	Spanish Colonial	Lindstrom-Anderson (c)
2064	1890	1968	5,000	Wm. A. Davern		J. P. Foglis
2078 (1)	1906	1955	4,000	Patrick Dougherty		John Entermann

List of Houses on Summit Avenue by Address

Address	Year Built	Year Razed or Moved	Estimated Cost	Original Owner	Style	Architect or Contractor (c)
2078 (2)	1955		300,000	Christ Child School	Contemporary	
2100	c.1956			Presently College of St. Thomas		
2106	1914	c.1956	5,000	Frank Nicolin, Jr.		Wm. Weise (c)
2110	1923		12,000	Harry Simpkin	Early Mod. Rect.	
2115				College of St. Thomas		
2120	1924		15,000	Walter Butler	Tudor Villa	Butler Bros. Co. (c)
2130	1918		5,500	Edna Glass	Twenties Villa	Edna Glass
2134	1921		4,000	Michael M. Tierney	Bungalow	
2140	1938		5,000	Mrs. O'Gorman	Bungalow	Emil Nelson (c)
2144	1931		7,500	Helen C. Smith		
2150	1918		5,000	McAnulty Co.	Bungalow	McAnulty Co. (c)
2154	1912		3,500	H. A. Folson		Jos. Fisby (c)
2156	1913		5,000	A. A. Klemner	Simplified Rect.	A. G. Erickson
2166	1950		17,000	Ernest J. Murphy	Bungalow	Wm. Golla (c)
2170	1922		10,000	H. S. Mills	Georgian Revival variant	O. H. Round

Address	Year Built	Year Razed or Moved	Estimated Cost	Original Owner	Style	Architect or Contractor (c)
2174	1921		8,500	S. Tierney	Early Mod. Rect.	F. K. Tewes (?)
2183	1925		9,000	Perry-Tryle Co.		Perry-Tryle Co. (c)
2187	1923		9,000	Ethel Karon	E. M. Georgian Rev.	
2195	1925		8,000	Jos. F. Rosenthal	Early Mod. Rect.	H. F. Thamert (c)
2215	1927		26,000	Archibald Bush	Tudor Villa	G. A. Anderson (c)
2225	1923		11,000	J. W. Gover	Tudor Villa	Mather & Fleischbein
2233	1923		12,000	E. J. Kingston	E. M. Georgian Rev.	Mather & Fleischbein
2241	1955		30,000	R. O. Bishop	Contemporary	Ellerbe & Co.
2249	1951		28,000	Chas. Coddon	Contemporary	Norman Johnson
2259	1922		14,000	D. E. V. Goltz	Georgian Revival	F. O. Peterson (c)
2265	1922		28,000	Geo. W. Robinson	Georgian Revival	Mather & Fleischbein
2279	1964		40,000	Geo. L. Burg	Contemporary	Assoc. Arch. & Engineers
2260				St. Paul Seminary		

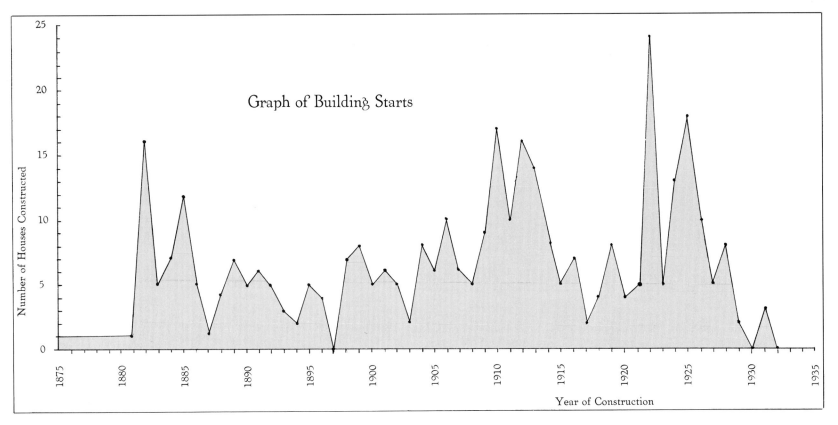

Graph of Building Starts

Number of Houses Constructed

Year of Construction

List of Houses on Summit Avenue by Year of Construction

1855	242, 288
1857	260, 266
1858	294, 312, 410
1862	432
1863	378, 226, 323
1866	251
1867	236
1869	252
1870	229
1872	624
1873	629
1874	217, 649
1875	360
1876	442
1877	435
1878	235
1879	540
1880	275
1881	495
1882	236, 239, 245, 271, 285, 301, 315, 345, 353, 361, 400, 415, 520, 534, 421, 201
1883	476, 243, 615, 475, 445
1884	266, 276, 288, 366, 555, 490, 255
1885	265, 295, 525, 659, 1494, 1586, 1596, 1620, 1624, 401, 403, 516
1886	226, 322–24, 344, 465, 545, 1722
1887	251

1888	240, 541, 710, 749
1889	302, 332, 587–601, 644, 665, 669, 1374
1890	596–604, 929, 1325, 1373, 2064
1891	261, 365, 513, 1003, 1093, 1127
1892	323, 335, 656, 760, 650
1893	318, 684, 779
1894	340, 638
1895	329, 579, 683, 985, 1317
1896	629, 505, 435, 623
1898	339, 442, 550, 701, 705, 842, 846
1899	285, 624, 937, 943, 1352, 1364, 1381, 1382
1900	672, 768, 1255, 1345–47, 1411
1901	275, 776, 1111, 965, 1009, 1035
1902	260, 533, 755, 966, 1118
1903	726, 808
1904	500, 574, 761, 955, 986, 1149, 1473, 1591
1905	301, 786, 1126, 1135, 1481, 1605
1906	807, 934, 1034, 1446, 1464, 1515, 1567, 1617, 1726, 1834, 2078
1907	485, 1156, 1410, 1510, 1635, 1850
1908	942, 1414, 1516, 1575, 1713
1909	345, 611, 780, 1180, 1190, 1220, 1376, 1493, 1732, 1740
1910	821, 1006, 1366, 1434, 1487, 1525, 1705, 1773, 1798, 1800, 1883, 1897, 1982, 2004, 2010, 796, 790

1911	370, 996, 1079, 1106, 1209, 1490, 1504, 1683, 1825, 1912, 1950
1912	361, 421, 834, 1142, 1456, 1731, 1749, 1826, 1858, 1866, 1873, 1936, 1944, 2022, 2052, 2154
1913	590, 739, 797, 1400, 1425, 1543, 1737, 1788, 1943, 1978, 1994, 2020, 2156
1914	516, 952, 1164, 1440, 1576, 1623, 1812, 1846, 1988
1915	344, 1027, 1179, 1725, 1770
1916	818, 990, 1186, 1761, 1818, 1855, 1987
1917	1789, 1995
1918	1358, 1415, 2130, 2150
1919	294, 470, 700, 706, 1141, 1428, 1953, 2048
1920	1042, 1046, 1335, 1559
1921	1200, 1838, 2015, 1921, 2174
1922	726, 862–864, 866–868, 1088, 1096, 1205, 1211, 1213, 1390, 1397, 1459, 1484, 1501, 1509, 1645, 1649, 1760, 1774, 1844, 1865, 1935, 2170, 2259, 2265
1923	894, 1393, 2110, 2225, 2233
1924	977, 1157, 1285, 1396, 1665, 1750, 1894, 1959, 1979, 2007, 2056, 2120, 2005

1925	660, 666, 1153, 1171, 1420, 1439, 1445, 1537, 1583, 1719, 1896, 1917, 1926, 1941, 1969, 2029, 2195
1926	573, 635, 1206, 1465, 1753, 1890, 1916, 1923, 1889, 1906
1927	608, 616, 1165, 1365, 2215
1928	366, 926, 1831, 1874, 1902, 1905, 2037, 1911
1929	1451, 1480
1931	1884, 1920, 2144
1936	2036, 2045
1938	1801, 1811, 1815, 2140
1948	615
1949	2038, 1837
1950	2166
1951	2249, 1795
1952	1389
1954	435, 828, 1353
1955	2241, 1964
1956	1212, 828
1957	1799
1959	1068
1960	1489, 1289, 1297, 854
1963	696
1964	2279
1966	456
1970	1845
1977	362–364

List of Houses on Summit Avenue by Style

*indicates that the house is no longer standing.

Italian Villa

1855	242*
1857	312
1858	294 (1)*
1862	432
1863	378*

Tuscan Villa

1875	360*
1877	435 (1)*
1882	271, 345*
1885	525*
1886	545*

Second Empire

1867	236 (1)*
1874	649
1882	201 (1)*
1883	243*

1870s–1880s Vernacular

1878	235 Second Empire
1882	301 (1)* Second Empire
1880s	1189 Stick
1885	1586*, 1596*, 1620*, 1624*, 1722 all Stick style

Queen Anne

1881	495
1882	236 (2)*, 353, 400, 445
1883	475
1884	255, 276*, 366*, 555*
1885	265, 295, 659
1886	465, 344 (1)*, 354
1888	749
1889	302, 665, 669, 1374
1890	929
1891	513
1899	624

Romanesque

1883	476, 490
1884	288*
1886	251, 322–24, 226 (2)*
1887	240
1889	332, 587–601
1890	596–604
1892	323, 760*
1893	318, 684

Beaux Arts — Eclectic

1891	261 Medieval
1894	340 It. Renaissance
1900	1345–1347 Dutch
1902	260 (2) Georgian, 533 It. Renaissance
1903	808 It. Renaissance
1905	301 (2) Georgian
1909	370 Georgian

1910	821 (2) Tudor, 1006 Tudor
1912	421 (2) It. Renaissance
1914	516 (2) It. Renaissance
1915	344 (2) It. Renaissance
1922	1649 It. Renaissance
1924	977 Federal Rev.
1928	366 (2) Georgian
1936	2045 Fr. Chateau

Rectilinear

1889	644 Queen Anne
1890	1373 Georgian, remodeled (?)
1891	365 Queen Anne, 1003 Queen Anne, later remodeled
1892	335 Queen Anne, 650 Georgian, 656 Georgian
1894	623 Medieval, 638 Queen Anne
1895	329 Queen Anne, 985 Queen Anne, 1317 Queen Anne
1896	435 (2) Queen Anne, 505 Medieval, 629 Medieval
1898	339 Medieval, 701 Medieval, 705 Medieval, 842 Queen Anne, 846 Queen Anne
1899	285 Georgian, 937 Queen Anne, 943 Georgian, 1352 Queen Anne, 1364 Queen Anne, 1381 Simplified, 1382 Queen Anne
1900	768 Queen Anne, 1189 Simplified, 1411 Simplified
1901	275 Medieval, 776 Queen Anne, 1009 Queen Anne
1902	755*, 966 Queen Anne, remodeled, 1118 Georgian
1903	726 Simplified
1904	761 Eclectic, 955 Jacobean, 986 Queen Anne, 1149 Simplified, 1344 Queen Anne, 1473 Simplified, 1591 Queen Anne
1905	786 Queen Anne, 1135 Eclectic, 1481 Medieval, 1605 Queen Anne
1906	790 Queen Anne, 796 Simplified, 934 Queen Anne, 1034 Medieval, 1446 Simplified, 1464 Medieval, 1515 Queen Anne, 1617 Simplified, 1726 Simplified, 1834 Simplified
1907	1156 Classical, 1510 Queen Anne, 1850 Simplified, 1635 Simplified
1908	942 Eclectic, 1414 Tudor, 1516 Queen Anne, 1575 Georgian
1909	611 Tudor, 780 Queen Anne, 1220 Simplified, 1376 Early Modern, 1732 Simplified

1910	574 Medieval, 1705 Simplified, 1798 Simplified, 1800 Simplified, 1982 Early Modern
1911	1825 Simplified, 1912 Early Modern
1912	506 Georgian, 692 Simplified, 1873 Early Modern, 2022 Early Modern (Prairie)
1913	590 Early Modern (Prairie), 1737 Simplified, 1788 Simplified, 2020 Early Modern, 2156 Simplified
1914	1164 Medieval, 1812 Tudor, 1846 Simplified
1915	1027 Simplified, 1179 Simplified, 1621 Tudor, 1761 Tudor
1916	1818 Early Modern, 1855 Classical
1917	1995 Simplified
1918	1358 Simplified
1920	1559 Early Modern
1921	1200 Early Modern, 2174 Early Modern
1922	1088, 1205 Early Modern, 1213 Early Modern, 1211 Early Modern, 1484 Early Modern, 1501 Early Modern, 1509 Early Modern, 1760 Early Modern, 1844 Early Modern, 1865 Early Modern, 1935 Early Modern
1923	2110 Early Modern
1924	2005 Early Modern
1925	660 Early Modern, 666 Early Modern, 1171 Early Modern, 1439 Early Modern, 1445 Early Modern, 1926 Early Modern, 2195 Early Modern
1926	1916 Early Modern

Georgian Revival

1895	683
1901	965, 1111*
1904	500
1910	1486, 1525
1911	1504
1912	834 Variant, 1142, 1858
1913	1017, 1425 Early Modern
1915	1725 Early Modern, 1770 Early Modern
1916	990
1917	1789
1919	294 (2), 1428 Early Modern, 1953 Early Modern, 2048 Early Modern
1920	1325

1921	2015
1922	862–64, 866 Variant, 1390, 1459, 1645, 2170, 2265
1923	2187, 2233
1924	1285, 1396, 1979, 2007
1925	1420 Early Modern, 1537, 1583 Early Modern, 1568, 1644, 1695, 2055
1926	1206 Early Modern, 1465, 1890
1927	1165
1938	1801, 1811

Tudor Villa

1905	1126
1906	1567, 807
1907	485, 1410
1908	1713
1909	345, 1180, 1493, 1740
1910	1403, 1434, 1773, 1883, 1897, 2004, 2010
1911	976, 1106, 1490, 1683
1912	361, 1134, 1456, 1747, 1826, 1936, 1944
1913	1400, 1543, 1943, 1978
1914	952, 1440, 1576
1915	1082
1916	818, 1987
1919	1141
1920	1046
1922	1774
1923	2225
1924	1157, 1665, 1894, 1959, 2120
1925	1719, 1779, 1969
1926	1753, 1923, 1365
1927	2215
1928	1874
1929	1451, 1480
1936	2032

Twenties Villa

1913	1994
1912	1731
1918	2130
1921	1838
1923	1393
1924	1750
1925	1153, 1896, 1917, 1941
1926	573, 1889
1928	1902, 1911, 2037

Spanish Colonial

1919	470
1924	2056
1925	2029
1928	1905, 1831
1931	1884, 1920

Index of Architects

Ernest R. Sandeen was the James Wallace Professor of History and codirector of the Living Historical Museum at Macalester College. He won distinction as a historian of religion and as an architectural historian, serving as a member of St. Paul's Historic Preservation Commission and as a partner in Lanegran, Richter, and Sandeen, an architectural preservation, design, and land-use firm. He is coauthor, with David A. Lanegran, of *The Lake District of Minneapolis: A History of the Calhoun–Isles Community,* also available from the University of Minnesota Press.

Larry Millett recently retired as a writer and critic for the *St. Paul Pioneer Press* but continues to write a column on architecture for the newspaper. He is the author of several books, including *Lost Twin Cities, Twin Cities Then and Now,* and a series of mystery novels featuring Sherlock Holmes.